Teaching the Unteachable

Teaching the Unteachable

PRACTICAL IDEAS TO GIVE TEACHERS HOPE AND HELP WHEN BEHAVIOUR MANAGEMENT STRATEGIES FAIL

Marie Delaney

www.worthpublishing.com

First published 2009 by Worth Publishing Ltd
9 Charlotte Road, London SW13 9QJ
www.worthpublishing.com

Reprinted 2015

Printed and bound by CPI Group (UK) Ltd, Croydon, CR0 4YY

British Library Cataloguing in Publication Data
A catalogue record for this book is available from the British Library

ISBN 9781903269121

Cover and text design by Anna Murphy
Front cover image: © Image Source/Getty Images

To my Mum and Dad
who always believed in me

Acknowledgements

To: The many children and young people with whom I have worked over the last twenty years. They have never ceased to amaze me, teach me and entertain me with their resilience, humour and perseverance. It is from them that I have learned the most. They are not mentioned here by name but they are the main inspiration for this book.

The colleagues who have helped me develop ideas and who have been prepared to try them out in difficult circumstances. Firstly: Paul Hill and Caitlin Walker at DYP for believing in me and supporting my early efforts with the 'unteachables'.

My many colleagues at Pilgrims Teacher Training, from whom I have learned so much about training and teaching. In particular to Simon Marshall for reading the first drafts of this book, Judy Baker for her help with NLP and Paul Davis for his creative ideas and continuing encouragement.

The staff at the Aveley School, who had to put up with my 'trial and error' approach and at times my own bad behaviour in my attempts to find solutions for the most challenging of pupils. In particular, to Julie Blevins for her friendship and commitment to 'giving it a go', to Debbie Perry, Lynda Martin, Cath Old and Linda Noble, for going well beyond the call of duty in their work in the LDC, Maggie Woodfield and Maggie Sanders for beginning the whole process.

The staff and pupils at Bower Park School, who were open to new ideas and prepared to take a risk on them. In particular, Mary Morrison and Mary Higgins for their remarkable vision, perserverance, stamina and belief in the value of this work. Also to Katie Conquest, Melanie Nash and Bev Mason for putting children first and always being willing to try out even the most unconventional ideas.

The Learning Mentors and staff in the Havering Excellence Cluster who put most of these ideas into practice and developed them beyond my own initial musings. In particular, Angie Brown for her unshakeable belief in the goodness of children and her capacity for seeing the best in everyone.

Shona Anderson for letting me be in 'her gang' and her unswerving conviction that change was possible.

Carol McWeeney for her faith in me, great PR and good humour as a training partner.

Lecturers and fellow students at the Caspari Foundation, from whom I learned that therapy has something to offer education, in particular Mia Beaumont for her insightful supervision, Heather Geddes for her inspiration, Gill Salmon for realising I didn't really want to give up, Michael Reeves and Susi Weatherall for their willingness to share ideas and remaining normal throughout the whole course.

Jessica Nash for reminding me why we left the bank and what's important about being a teacher.

New colleagues in Ireland who have been prepared to take a risk, even when the results were not always immediately obvious - in particular, Aileen Lyons, Paul Murphy, Sharon Lambert, Maria Nyhan-Hayes, Louise O'Keeffe and Emma Terry.

My family, Mum, Dad, and Jen for their continuing love, belief in me and unwavering support, and of course, Aidan.

Olly - for putting up with my bad moods as I failed to meet deadlines and blamed it on him.

Andrea Perry for her superb editing and being able to make sense of the first draft.

Martin Wood of Worth Publishing, for recognising the potential writer in me and his complete commitment to the ideas in this book.

Marie Delaney is an educational psychotherapist, teacher and teacher trainer. She has extensive experience of working with challenging behaviour - from both staff and pupils! She has worked on outside school projects - at DYP, a Mentoring and Education programme in Hackney, London - as well as in schools as a Learning Support Unit manager in Thurrock, and then as Learning Mentor/LSU co-ordinator for primary and secondary schools in Havering. She was also a trainer and moderator on the National Training for Learning Mentors. She works as Emotional Literacy Manager in a secondary school in Essex. Marie has trained teachers in the UK and abroad, and is now the Director of The Learning Harbour, Crosshaven, Co. Cork. Her main interests are introducing therapeutic approaches into mainstream schools to develop realistic strategies for challenging behaviour. She runs workshops and training programmes for all educational staff and related agencies.

NOTES ABOUT THE BOOK

1. To protect the confidentiality of individual children, carers or professionals, names and autobiographical details have been altered in every case quoted. Any case examples written are composite and drawn from a number of similar examples known to the Author from her experiences over many years of working with children and adolescents.
2. To simplify the text, the male gender is used on occasion to represent the child or young person, and the female gender to represent educational staff. No prejudice implied by this.
3. To simplify the text, the term '*child*' has been used on occasion to represent both children and young people. The strategies described are relevant to both primary and secondary phases, unless stated otherwise.
4. To simplify the text, the term '*parent*' is used on occasion to represent those now providing the primary care for children or young people. This term will therefore include adoptive parents, foster carers, family and friends.

Contents

(continues ...)

Contents (continued)

Chapter 1

...And I thought I was a good teacher!

Things had reached crisis point in the year 11 French class. John, a fifteen year old who was considered by most teachers to be de-motivated and difficult to teach, had just picked up his books, stormed towards the door and shouted "That's fine then, I'll go, I know when I'm not wanted". I - the behavioural management and emotional literacy expert - shot back, equally angrily, "Good, you've finally got the message" - and flung open the door.

As John charged out of the class, slamming the door behind him, I saw that a senior member of staff was walking past and smiling ruefully. I was embarrassed to think that she had witnessed such a public display of poor classroom management. This same member of staff confided in me later that she was secretly pleased that sometimes I couldn't deal with certain pupils any better than anyone else. She said that at times, she too felt completely useless and incompetent when she could not find solutions for some of the more challenging children in her year group.

There are days when some children can seem completely unteachable and we feel completely de-skilled as teachers. We feel that we cannot understand or reach them. Having trained as a teacher and then later as an educational psychotherapist, I became interested in why this happens. What is happening on those days when we feel like packing it all in and getting a job in the local supermarket? Why does it seem so simple when specialists show or tell us how to do it, and then so difficult when we try? Does anyone write about their failures, the days when it all seems too much?

This book represents the development of my own thoughts and ideas over years of working with children and young people who are at risk of being excluded from schools, and with the staff who are trying to find ways to teach them. I have run trainings for hundreds of teachers and support staff over the years, and I have found very few people who are not aware of the basics of good classroom management. What is interesting is why these strategies are so hard to apply in some situations and with some children.

I believe it happens in part because as teachers dealing at times with very troubled children, not enough attention is paid to our own emotions and how constant challenges can make us feel. The other side of this equation is trying to understand what is happening with these 'unteachable' children, to block their ability to learn. We may all have different interpretations of a pupil who is regarded as unteachable, but in general I am assuming that these children and young people display some of the following behaviours, on a regular basis, across different classes. Such pupils tend to -

→ react negatively to changes in routine or teaching staff
→ show physically or verbally aggressive behaviour to staff or other pupils
→ show aggressive behaviour in response to classroom pressures
→ become excessively withdrawn in reaction to any of the above
→ react inappropriately to correction or praise
→ have a poor ability to sustain relationships with peers
→ persistently break the school rules
→ exhibit constant low levels of off-task behaviour
→ exhibit excessive mood swings
→ go to extreme lengths to attract attention
→ provoke or distract other pupils from their work

→ persistently truant
→ present behaviour likely to injure themselves, other pupils, and staff, or damage equipment

To understand why this happens, it must first be recognised that teachers are only human! There will be days and times when even the things on this list are easier to deal with. Before looking at any strategies for managing difficult situations, I would like to look at how our own feelings play a part in our capacity to cope with this extremely challenging behaviour.

WHY TEACHERS' FEELINGS MATTER

In general, even the most challenging children come into school every day and pretty much do the same things. Some days they seem more responsive to our methods than others. Some pupils are in general more responsive than others. However, what makes a huge difference tends to be the responses of the adults around them. Something which may seem manageable at the start of term when we are fit, rested and feeling positive, seems overwhelming later in the year when we are tired and worn-down, worrying about test and exam results.

Bradley - an example of low-level confrontation

Bradley is thirteen and usually comes into class late, having overslept and missed the bus. He nearly always has a cap on when he enters the class, even though he knows it is against school rules.

On one Monday his English teacher, Mrs Fisher, smiles when she sees him, indicates he should sit down, continues with her lesson and when he has settled, gives him a non-verbal signal to remind him to take his cap off. After some comments to his friends, he sits down and takes the cap off.

Two weeks later, Mrs Fisher has had an unplanned late night, been delayed in traffic, rushed into school, found out she has to cover a colleague's lesson in her free period and has just seen a pupil in the corridor whom the Head had promised staff would be permanently excluded. Bradley comes in and the teacher immediately tells him angrily that she is sick of him coming in late and flounting school rules. She tells him to take off the cap and sit down without making a fuss. Bradley begins to argue with her about the cap and where he has to sit, finally muttering "Alright, keep your wig on!" The teacher explodes, and calls for Senior Management to remove Bradley from the class.

We are told that good teaching involves not taking it personally. However, at times like this, it can all feel very personal!

WHOSE FEELINGS AND BEHAVIOUR MADE THE REAL DIFFERENCE?

In both scenarios above, the pupil did more or less what he does every day. It was the teacher's reaction which was different, and this was affected by her own emotional and physical state. When discussing the incident afterwards, Mrs Fisher struggled to understand why her usually good class management had broken down on this occasion.

"Usually I think I manage my classes quite well. I have routines, clear rules and sanctions. I realise it is important to develop a good relationship with my pupils and try to see them as individuals. I have been observed teaching difficult classes and got positive feedback from the observers.

And yet, if I am having a bad day myself, I can sometimes feel completely incompetent with Bradley. He just pushes all my buttons and I end up shouting at him, being sarcastic or having him removed from class - all the things I know don't work with him."

Things had conspired against Mrs Fisher on that particular day to make it seem impossible to react appropriately. Teachers are only human and our responses, particularly to challenging behaviour, will be affected by our own emotional and physical states.

Teachers' feelings DO matter, and we need to be able to reflect on our own feelings without worrying that to do so is a sign of failure or a waste of time (*see more on* p.54). We need to give ourselves permission to try to understand ourselves and our feelings, before we can understand those of the challenging children we teach.

PAUSE FOR THOUGHT

Take a moment and write down the emotions you went through yesterday at work

I am sure you'll have noted a roller-coaster of emotions, ranging from positive feelings, even elation, all the way through to despair. Whenever I run seminars for teachers and ask them to do this, an avalanche of emotions and thoughts is released. Generally schools are not places where we are encouraged to notice and reflect on how we are feeling. There never appears to be time for that!

In this book I hope to give you time to reflect on what is happening to you when you are dealing with these challenging children. I will look at some of the conscious and unconscious processes which can affect our readiness for teaching and learning; understanding these will increase the likelihood of success.

AND WHAT ABOUT THOSE 'UNTEACHABLE' CHILDREN?

Our feelings as teachers do sometimes affect our ability to manage classes. However, there are also those children and young people who are very difficult to reach and deal with at any time. Even when we are motivated and teaching well, these children can present problems in our classes. They do not seem to respond to 'good' teaching methods. These children have usually had traumatic lives, with experience of trauma, loss, separation, neglect, abuse and violence. They come into school most days with their minds pre-occupied by anxieties, fears and worries. School may be the only place which is predictable and safe. This does not mean these children and young people will behave well and do what we ask. In fact, the opposite may be true - because school is the safe place, they will 'act out' and test boundaries. These pupils will test our inner resources and self-confidence more than any others.

In this book, I will offer you insights based on ideas from educational psychotherapy on how to understand and work with these children and young people. There are no 'magic' solutions, much as we would like there to be. However, by trying to gain an insight into their worlds, we might be able to offer them some hope at engaging in education. These are the pupils whom Barrett & Trevitt (1991) describe as -

> ...children who 'just can't get started'... those who 'get stuck'...those who seem deliberately to 'get it wrong' and rubbish their work. These children are apparently unable to come to terms with what is required of them in school. This can result in teachers becoming distressed and frustrated, *leaving them to doubt their own skills.* (p.1) *my emphasis*

In my experience, it is a relief to realise that sometimes it is what these children 'do to us' that makes us doubt our competence. Accepting this is an integral part of being able to work with them and develop more effective learning environments. Such pupils cannot just be *'fixed'* by yet more good behaviour management strategies.

In summary

This is a book for classroom teachers who would like to expand their ways of dealing with challenging, troubled children

- There is a wealth of good advice on behaviour management strategies which can be used to deal with challenging pupils. Chapter 2 will present a summary of those I have found most useful.
- There are times when even the best of these behaviour management strategies do not work, and this book will explore what might be happening at those times. It will look at what happens to teachers and what is going on for these 'unteachable' pupils (Chapters 3-5)
- As teachers, we need to be aware of and take care of our own emotions and feelings. Our emotional and physical state affects our ability to teach and deal with challenge effectively
- Children who have experienced trauma, loss, neglect, abuse and violence may have difficulties in class which are exhibited in seemingly inexplicable behaviour
- These children can make the adults around them feel de-skilled and incompetent

(continues ...)

- We need to be able to maintain our own capacity to think around these children
- By understanding some of the theory from educational psychotherapy (Chapters 6-9), we can develop more strategies for dealing with these complex cases in class and in school (Chapters 10-12)

Chapter 2

But what are those tried-and-tested Behaviour Management Strategies?

It is worth remembering that the majority of children respond well to consistency, clear rules, boundaries and fairness. When we are feeling frustrated and annoyed about our classes, we tend to lose sight of this fact. Most teachers report that it is the low-level, continually disruptive behaviour (talking off-task, chewing gum, passing notes, being slow to follow rules) which can be wearing and grind them down. Although frustrating, pupils demonstrating these types of behaviour will, in most cases, respond to clear and consistent classroom management. In this chapter, before focusing on the children who present us with the most complex challenges, I will outline what I mean by clear and consistent classroom management.

I will summarise the kinds of tips I have found useful throughout my career as a classroom teacher and trainer. They have been collected from a broad and diverse range of sources and colleagues, and are based on ideas which seem to work for most people, with most students, most of the time. Some of these suggestions will be familiar to you and some may be less well known. They can be considered as an addition to your 'toolkit' of classroom management strategies - to dip into and try out as required to address the issues described. You will also find some space for personal reflection, time to think about the issues described. These 'pauses for thought' could also be used as discussion points with colleagues or in training sessions.

ISSUE 1: PREPARING YOURSELF TO MEET THE CLASS

✔ Creating positive expectations in yourself

Our attitude and state of mind can greatly influence the impact we have on a class and their behaviour. In every school, there is a class which everyone dreads, full of students who take on demon-like characteristics in our minds. We have all had these classes. They are usually called something like 8B3 or 9B4 and seem to be timetabled on Fridays last period, or after PE, when the students all come in late, over-excited and difficult to settle. How we choose to think about these classes will influence what happens. Do we, often without realising it, begin with a lot of sharp commands, or do we start with something positive?

> PAUSE FOR THOUGHT
>
> **Think about how you might walk into a challenging class**
>
> Would you be thinking - "*Oh no, not them again, I can't wait for the bell*"?
>
> Now think about how you would walk into the room if it were one of your favourite classes, a class who responds to your instructions, can have fun and work. Imagine yourself walking in, as if you were thinking,
>
> "*Thank goodness it is 8A2, they did some really nice work last week*".

Your thoughts about the class will inevitably have an influence on how you enter the room. This in turn will have an impact on the pupils' reactions to you and your teaching. They will respond accordingly. If our body language indicates that we would rather be somewhere else, the pupils will want to be somewhere else as well! As Katie, a thirteen year old says:

"You really know when a teacher doesn't like teaching your class. You can even tell by the way they look at you or just sigh when you ask them something. If they don't like me, why should I bother to do what they want me to do?"

- Before a difficult class, find something positive to focus on, and walk in as if you were looking forward to teaching this class. Plan what you are going to say in the first three minutes, so that your initial comments are positive rather than negative. Saying "*Right you lot, let's see if we can have a better lesson than last week, we might even get some work done today*" already frames a negative assumption about our expectations of the class. So perhaps instead we could try saying, "*Right, building on the good work done last week, I thought we would get on and finish this project today. I know this group is capable of it*".

It might seem strange and almost untrue, but it creates an expectation and an aspiration. Difficult classes have a way of living down to our expectations, and we need to bring them up.

✔ Being aware of your own state in the room and the state you are creating

What is the best emotional and physical state for teaching and learning? What state do you need to be in, and what state do you want your students to be in?

PAUSE FOR THOUGHT

Think about what you need to get yourself into the best state for teaching

What is a resourceful state for you personally?
Relaxed? Energised? Focused?

How do you know when you are in this state?

What are you seeing, hearing and feeling?

Envisage a time when you were in this state, and think about the factors which influenced it.

Can you create some of these factors for yourself before your lesson?

Maggie, a History teacher, said in relation to this question:

> *"Sometimes, when I feel totally stressed, I need to go into the cupboard in my room and just yell. It sounds crazy, but it releases all my pent-up emotion and I can be in a calm state for my next class. Also, I find it helps to snatch a moment with my colleague to 'let off steam' in breaks".*

Joe, a Newly Qualified Teacher (NQT):

> *"I have a postcard of the beach where I got married. Looking at it cheers me up and puts more positive thoughts in my head. I keep it behind my desk, where I can see it easily"*

✔ Preparing the climate in the classroom

Beginnings are of vital importance. Although it is possible to recover from a bad start, it can be an uphill struggle. It is easier to try to set up the beginning properly. This will involve setting expectations and classroom rules and responsibilities.

- Rules need to be few, clear and positive. If possible, discuss them with the class and make sure everyone is clear about why a rule is important. Circle Time games can be a good way to introduce the rules and the reasons for them. And then keep to them. If you start well and then lapse, you are giving the unconscious message that the rules do not matter.
  (See Quality Circle Time in Secondary Schools, Moseley, 1996, David Fulton Publishing*) for ways to do this in secondary schools).*

- Learn names and the correct pronunciation as soon as possible. It can make all the difference to some students to know that you know how to pronounce their names and what they liked to be called. If you have a problem remembering names, write them phonetically on a seating plan to help you get started.

✔ Starting the class

Again, be aware of the states you are creating in the room. For example, if you pace around restlessly whilst giving instructions, are you energising the class, or are you adding to the agitation and restlessness of those students who find it difficult to focus?

- Think about your body language, and how you are standing in the classroom. Freeze your body when giving instructions, keeping your weight evenly distributed, and your toes forward for getting attention.

Pay attention to your breathing. Low, slow breathing is calming. It may help to practise consciously slowing your breathing as you enter the classroom and at regular intervals, and particularly if you notice you are becoming agitated. Be aware if you are holding your breath - we tend to do this when worried or facing a potential confrontation such as a challenging class.

- Standing in one place to give instructions can help. Match your actions with your instructions. For example, stand still to tell a class to stop an activity. Be consistent with your use of space. Don't give instructions for the next stage when you are walking to the front of the class. Most students will need to be looking at you to understand the task.

- Use the NLP (Neuro-Linguistic Programming) technique of anchoring. For example, have different places in the room where you stand, a place to give instructions, a place to discipline, a place to set homework. After a while, the class will unconsciously become aware of these and know what to expect when you move into a certain position.

- Use non-verbal anchors and cues to signal the beginning and ending of activities. For example, if students are about to engage in a noisy activity, we can agree in advance a non-verbal signal, such as dimming the lights, which will indicate that it is time to stop talking and focus on the teacher at the front. This will effectively stop the activity in a calm way, and does not involve the teacher shouting over the students.

- Have classroom posters for routines and rules - you will then only need to indicate the poster to remind the class if a rule is being broken.

- Use traffic lights or a barometer on the wall which can be moved or changed to indicate that the group is going off-task. Red would indicate completely off-task, amber would mean going off-task and green would indicate they are back on-task. Create a signal which means "*Stop what you are doing and listen*". Some teachers put a finger to their lips. I have found it useful to teach the class to watch for when I put my hand up. When they see this signal, they should put their hand up and stop talking. This can create a 'ripple of silence' effect.

- Use your voice as an auditory anchor. Use pauses and incomplete sentences for effect and to get attention rather than speaking over a rowdy class.
  (For more on anchoring and NLP, see In Your Hands, Revell & Norman, *1997, Saffire Press)*

- It goes without saying that we need to be prepared and on-time for class. It can then help to have an activity on the board which encourages students to come in, sit down and focus their attention visually. I have found it useful to put up a riddle, a word puzzle, or a sentence written backwards for students to look at and mull over. Look at the following examples:

DEVOWELLING	cn y rd th qstn?
BACKWARDS	noitseuqehtdaerouynac?
RUNITTOGETHER	canyoureadthequestion?

I have found that even the most disruptive students can quickly get interested in a brainteaser, and it saves us having to say repeatedly (and often more and more loudly) "*Sit down, be quiet.*" We can then speak quietly to any students who are not becoming engaged, and focus their attention onto the task.

- Respond to and acknowledge those students who have come into the classroom appropriately, rather than continually notice those who have not. You can do this individually:
  "Thank you, John, for settling so quickly"
  Or to groups:
  "This table is ready to work"
  "Well done to all of you for being on time today"
  With more challenging students it can help to make a comment which shows you remember them personally, for example:
  "Heard the football team did well last night, Joe, well done, can you sit over there, thanks".
  Such a comment distracts and shows that you can acknowledge the students, without them needing to play up.

✔ Keeping the focus on learning

In challenging classes a lot of discussion and attention is spent on directions and comments to do with behaviour.

"I need you to be quiet"
"This class is behaving terribly and I will not put up with it."

- Wherever possible, link the reason for your directions to the learning:
  "OK, there's a lot of noise in here at the moment which is making it difficult to think"
  "We are all responsible for keeping a good learning climate and we need to think about how to do this"

- Use the first lesson to show your teaching style and ways of managing. Choose a topic you are comfortable with and enjoy. This will get you further with a challenging class than being a slave to the scheme of work. Students need to see you teaching at your best and in your best frame of mind, and this is far easier if you are sure about the content of the lesson.

ISSUE 2: KEEPING IT FLOWING IN CLASS

✓ Using constructive language

Your own use of language is of vital importance and can consciously or unconsciously affect the thinking in the room. It can be useful to:

- Tell pupils what you want them to do, not what you don't want them to do. Our brains process the negative by thinking of the positive and negating it. For example, if I say to you "*Don't think of a blue tree!*" - what do you think of? Most of us think of a blue tree and then negate it. Similarly, if you tell a student not to do something, their brains will consider doing it and quite possibly they will start doing it, without necessarily intending to be difficult!

- Chunk instructions, give them on a need-to-know basis, and not in a long list at the beginning of an activity. Demonstrate and use visuals wherever possible.

- Avoid the use of sequencers where possible. For example, if you say "*Before you open your books, I want you to look at the board*", the brain will hear "*Open your books*" and organise itself to follow that instruction. Instead, say - "*First I want you to look at the board*".

- Where possible give action words last. This will be the word students will remember if they are not good listeners or are finding it difficult to pay attention. For example, you might say: "*OK, I'll play the dialogue again, ready? Listen.*"

- Use "*and*" instead of the word "*but*". For example, if I say - "*I can understand you think it isn't fair, but you need to do the homework again*", the brain does not hear the first part of the sentence, it only hears the negative second part. If instead, I say - "*I can understand you think it isn't fair, and you do need to do the homework again*" - there is some chance that the brain will hear the positive and be reassured that not everything is negative.

- Give some kind of perceived choice if possible. For example, you can say - "*We need to cover this section, and you can do it on this sheet or in your books.*"

  Many students who disrupt classes react negatively to what they perceive as direct commands. By building in a choice which keeps the task in mind, we allow them to have some independence, but also to get our task done.

- Show through your language that you expect your instruction to be followed. Add "*thank you*" to the end of a directive. It creates the idea that you expect the directive to be followed. Keep your tone polite and pleasant though! For example, "*John, can you move over there, thank you.*"

- If you want to get attention, it can be useful to say, "*Can you show me you are listening?*". This is more effective than simply saying "*Listen*".

There will be students who will argue with you that they can listen and talk at the same time. The issue here is that they need to show you that they are listening in a way you can understand.

✔ Practising using silence

- Use silence to get the attention of your class. Be prepared to wait for silence before you start speaking. Talking over a class is counter-productive and will set precedents. If you find yourself doing this with a disruptive class, you will be giving them the message that it does not matter if they are talking when you want silence.

- If possible, have signals which attract attention and get silence. Praise those who stop talking and show they are listening. "*Well done, this table is ready and showing me they are listening.*" This is a technique often used in primary but I have found it very effective with secondary groups, if used in a fairly humorous way.

ISSUE 3: PUTTING LEARNING BACK ON TRACK

✔ Keeping the tone positive

In even the best planned lessons, the unexpected will happen. Whenever I sit in a lecture at a conference, I am reminded how difficult it is to concentrate and behave for long periods of time!

- During the class, notice and acknowledge things which are going well. Give specific praise. General praise such as "*You are being good today*" does not teach children what the appropriate behaviour is. Instead, say something which highlights the observable behaviour: "*Well done for being patient and waiting your turn*". Always be polite, however tempting it is to say something sharp or sarcastic.

- It is important to notice when the child who often gets into trouble is showing the appropriate behaviour, even if this means noticing what they are NOT doing! For example, you might say to a child who has been continually interrupting in previous lessons - "*Thank you for listening without interrupting.*" Most children who behave badly at school say that they are no longer noticed when they start behaving appropriately. Noticing good behaviour and commenting on it teaches them that they can also get acknowledged for doing the right thing.

✔ Dealing with arguments

- If a student is getting into an argument with you, try to acknowledge that you can empathise with their view of the world. It may not be yours, and you don't have to agree with it, but acknowledging it will help. Listening to them does not mean you agree. For example, you might say - "*I can understand that you think you have done this before and don't understand the point of doing it again, and we still need to do it again to get the exam practice.*"

- Remember to keep the focus on the main purpose, the learning. We are often distracted into arguments about behaviour when the whole point is that we need to create and maintain learning environments together: "*OK, I hear what you are saying, and now what about number four, I think you have the answer?*"

- Use the broken record technique. Calmly repeat the instructions and wait. Walk towards the disruptive student when first talking to them, walk away with your eyes on them when they answer.

- Distract at the point of conflict. Most students are quite easily thrown off-track by an unexpected positive remark or a comment about something you know about them or their interests. For example, "*Jess, heard you were great in the sports day yesterday, didn't know you were such a good runner. I wonder if you could use some of that focus to help us here?*"
  Using this as an opener can take the pupil by surprise, allow you to regain some rapport and then deal with the issue.

- Give positive reinforcement as soon as possible after a conflict. Acknowledge that the student is now back on track, or any attempt they make to participate appropriately.

✔ Creating group responsibility for a learning climate

- Encourage the group to take responsibility for the learning climate. For example, ask them to mark themselves out of ten for the learning skills they used today. Questions you could build in as regular self-feedback are:

  → "*How well did I listen?*"
  → "*How well did I put my point of view across?*"
  → "*How well did I empathise with others?*"
  → "*How much effort did I put into the task?*"
  → ???

Ideally, you should also include yourself in this feedback! Encourage the group to see feedback as a necessary part of learning, and not criticism. Ask, "*What could we have done better to create an even better learning climate?*"
You may be surprised at the answers!

- In *Cracking the Hard Class* (1997, Paul Chapman), Rogers suggests running class meetings to re-focus on the need to keep to rules, respect rights and act responsibly. Students are encouraged to discuss good teaching, good learning and what rules there need to be to maintain this.

- Wherever possible, avoid public confrontations. If you need to remove a student from class, it is better to discuss the matter with them privately and without an audience of peers. It is easier to ask them to stay behind for a few minutes and discuss the issues than to be drawn into a public argument about their perceived attitude, for example.

✔ Holding the private conversation

It may be necessary to speak to a student privately about their behaviour. Before this happens, you might need to have them removed from your class, if their behaviour was completely inappropriate at that moment.

- Be clear what the school procedure is and who can help you. If your school has an on-call system, make sure you know how to use it if you need to have a student removed from your class. Even if you do ask for a student to be removed, you will need to deal with the matter yourself in order to be able to work with this child in future. However tempting it is to move the matter up the ladder of sanctions - particularly if the child has been in a lot of trouble with other people as well - you will not be gaining any credibility if you are not involved in sorting the problem out. What do you say?

- In a private conversation, you want to give the student a chance to feel listened to and to move onto a solution. Too often this type of conversation can become very negative and blaming. I have found it useful to use the three-sentences rule. Ask the student to take a moment and tell you in three sentences what has happened. This can be useful when sorting out disputes because it avoids long, protracted monologues, in which it becomes difficult for either party to focus on the main issue.

For example, Shanice has been asked to explain why she was fighting in class with Dawn:
"Miss, she started it, I was just sitting at my desk, minding my own business, when Sarah told me that Dawn was dissing me to my friends, just 'coz I was talking to John, who I know she's totally sweet on and now I know she's just jealous 'coz no-one likes her. And anyway, there I was, minding my own business, when she comes in and starts giving it, like, thinking she can, like as if she was one we should all listen to and I was thinking that Sarah might be right, but how did Dawn know anyway and..."

Shanice is asked to calm down and say what happened in three sentences:
"Well, I was sitting down and Sarah came in and started shouting at me. Said I was trying to get her boyfriend, John. That made me mad so I started shouting at her and Mrs Brown tried to stop us."

This means that we can begin to sort out the dispute, without the pupil working herself up into such a frenzy that she is unable to listen to what is being said.

- It can also be useful to use another NLP technique which is called 'stacking up 'yes' responses'. This means that you state several things at the beginning of your conversation which the student cannot disagree with. For example, you might say -
  "*Thanks for staying behind to sort this out. You know I asked you to stay behind because of what happened just now in class. I am sure neither of us want to be spending a lot of our own time arguing. We both need to find a way to get the work done*"
  These four statements will cause the student to agree with you internally. If you then add into this the idea of pacing their objections (*below*), you will start the conversation off in a positive way.

- Pacing objections simply means acknowledging, in your opening statements, any objections you think the student might have. For example, you might say -
  "*You probably think I am being unfair by asking only you to stay behind*". By naming the possible objection, you give the student less chance to use it as their opening gambit, and you show you are trying to understand their viewpoint.

- Look for solutions. Trying to make students say they are sorry can be a pointless exercise. What is more useful is to ask what they would do differently next time or what needs to happen next time. If you have a class contract, it can be useful to ask them what rule they were breaking. Explain that you want them to be part of a solution, not part of the problem.

- Focus on describing the inappropriate behaviour rather than your interpretation of it (*see below for more on interpretation*).
  Involve the student in the discussion and plan for intervention.
  "*If someone else was doing this, what would you advise?*"
  "*We need a solution here, what could we do?*"
  "*I'm trying to understand why this happened, can you help me?*"
  "*What could be the right behaviour here?*"

✔ Showing the students you are human

Remember things will go wrong. We are not perfect. Be prepared to admit to it and to model to students how to repair relationships. See 'failure' as an opportunity for you and the students to learn how to do it differently the next time. Be consistent, but admit when you are not.

- A useful way to do this is to say "*I think we both could have handled that differently. Let's think about what happened and what needs to happen to put it right*".
  In the example I described in Chapter 1, I needed to go back to the student and tell him that I had not handled things very well, that we needed to find a solution to the problem together. In fact he was quite happy with this, and had already thought of some suggestions himself.

✔ Separating behaviour from our judgement of the behaviour

We often talk about making a distinction between the student and his behaviour. You can like a student and not like his behaviour. This sounds easy in theory, but can be difficult in practice. Sean, a fourteen year old with whom I was working on this matter commented -

"That's all well and good, that teachers are told to separate who you are from your behaviour, but you really know if they don't like you!"
If we are honest, we might admit that Sean has a point.

PAUSE FOR THOUGHT

Take a moment and think about a student you have found difficult to deal with

Write a description of what it is that is annoying or difficult about them. Now divide your comments into two lists, those which describe a behaviour, and those which give your judgement of the behaviour.

In my experience of working with many teachers in workshops, there will be, inevitably, a lot of comments which focus on the interpretation of the behaviour. This is only natural, since, when we find ourselves in conflict, we often use our own filters and values to attach meaning and labels to behaviour. Unfortunately doing so can make it difficult to gain any rapport with these students. For example, do you think the following comments are descriptions of behaviour or a teacher's interpretation of the behaviour?

"He's not interested"
"He never pays attention"
"She doesn't listen"
"She's always trying to disrupt the lesson"

If we look at the language and think about these statements, they are not descriptions of behaviour. We do not know what the student is actually doing to cause the teacher to say this. How is he showing he is not interested? What is she doing that makes me think she is not listening?

This type of comment often provokes a very negative, confrontational attitude in the student, along the lines of -

"If you think that's what I am, that's what I will be"

or *"Of course I'm listening, prove I'm not".*

If we are specific in our description of the behaviour and separate it from our judgement of that behaviour, we will be able to discuss the situation more easily with a student. If I can describe specifically what the student is doing to make me think they are not paying attention, I can describe why, for example, that particular behaviour leads me to think they are not listening. For example, I might say - *"When you look out of the window when I am giving instructions, I think that you are not listening".* This is different to *"Stop looking out of the window and not listening".* The latter could cause a protracted argument about whether the student is listening or not, whereas the former explains it from my point of view and is harder to argue about!

✔ Finding a positive intention in the behaviour

A student who is looking out the window might not be listening. or might be thinking deeply about what the teacher just said. How can I know unless I can check it out with the student? The next step is to think of a possible positive intention to it. This is not easy to do with students with whom we are having conflict. For example, teachers sometimes say begrudgingly about a student who is calling out, *"I suppose they just want attention".* Most teachers don't believe that wanting attention is a positive thing in itself. I would suggest that the student may well think the teacher is the most important person in the room, and wants to show them they are interested. If I choose to think this, I could say something like -

> *"I think it's great that you want to show me you are interested and my opinion is important to you, and we need to find a way to give everyone a chance to answer. When you keep calling out without putting your hand*

up, it stops this happening. So I need you to try to remember to put your hand up and wait"

✔ Pacing and leading

Learn to match and pace the energy and mood of your group. If you are teaching last lesson on a Friday afternoon, your class may come in lethargic or restless and looking forward to the weekend. Saying something like *"OK, lets get on with it, open your books at page seventeen"* might create the opposite effect to the one you want. Try saying something like -

"OK, I know its Friday last lesson and you are tired and looking forward to the end of the day, let's see what we can do that will get us into the mood for learning".

This is an example of trying to match the students' mood and energy. Of course, then you want to lead to a better state and energy-level for learning.

✔ Using sanctions

Do not make idle threats. Sanctions need to be clearly stated and carried out if a student continues to misbehave.

→ Be clear why you are giving that sanction
→ Give sanctions for disruptive behaviours
→ Avoid public sanctions wherever possible
→ Make sanctions small and certain
→ Combine with positive reinforcement as soon as possible afterwards

In summary

This chapter looked at some key principles which can help with effective class management. Classroom management is about managing ourselves as well as the class, and we need to develop ways to do this

- Be aware of your own emotional and physical state. Check in with yourself and notice if you are in a resourceful state for teaching. If not, use strategies to get yourself into the best possible state

- Be aware of the states you are creating in your classroom with your body language, energy, tone of voice and use of language. Plan how to develop positive states

- Keep the focus on learning, rather than purely behaviour, and emphasise everyone's responsibility for maintaining a learning climate. If you can, discuss and agree these responsibilities with the class, and refer back to the discussion when you need to

- Have a few rules, but stick to them. Link them to the idea of rights and responsibilities

- Practise using precise language. Be solution-focused and look for positive intentions in behaviour so that you can re-frame it for yourself and the

(continues ...)

student. Avoid embedded commands, state what you want to happen, not what you don't want

- Describe the behaviour which is not appropriate, rather than your interpretation of it
- Be consistent. Admit when you are not
- Remember things will go wrong. We are not perfect. Show by your actions how to repair relationships. See 'failure' as an opportunity for you and the students to learn how to do it differently the next time
- Show empathy with a challenging student's position. It is not the same as agreeing that their behaviour is acceptable
- A lot of quick wins for both parties is better than striving for one big win
- Pace and lead. Start from where the pupils are to take them where you want to go
- It will sometimes be necessary to impose sanctions. Make them small and certain

Chapter 3

Well, I tried all those strategies and they're still unteachable!

WHAT IS GOING ON IN OUR CLASSES WHEN THESE METHODS APPEAR NOT TO WORK?

The ideas in the previous chapter are all valid behaviour management strategies. I have collected them over the years from various experts, colleagues, from theories and from my own experience. In general, they work well. I would be happy taking over the most difficult class with this 'toolkit' up my sleeve.

However, what happens when these ideas don't seem to be working? When tried and trusted methods meet with little success in our efforts to 'manage' some pupils' behaviour, we can end up feeling very de-motivated and defeated. These are the children and young people mentioned in the introduction - the pupils who have suffered trauma, loss, neglect, abuse and violence. They may seem unresponsive or unpredictable in their responses to our teaching - in fact, 'unteachable'.

When our best efforts to teach these pupils in mainstream classrooms repeatedly meet with failure, we usually react in one of two ways.

1 We can find ourselves feeling frustrated at our lack of success and continual battles with the child or young person. We can find ourselves thinking: *"There's absolutely nothing more I can do to help Josh, nothing I am trying is working, no-one can teach him and he is stopping others from learning. We can't keep him in this school, he should be permanently excluded and I can get on with the job of teaching those who are teachable."*

2 Even if we do not harbour such punitive feelings about the pupil, we can still feel at a loss about how to manage him in our class. We might find ourselves thinking:
"I know Josh has a lot of problems and a terrible home life, but we don't have the specialist skills here to deal with him. It would be much better for him to be taught by real specialists, they could really help him. We are only failing him here, there must be somewhere better able to deal with him."

Understandable as both these reactions may be, the end result is the same. Children who have spent their life being rejected are then rejected by the school and 'float around' the education system.

Unfortunately, exclusion from our classes and schools does not usually create any solutions for these children or for society. The truth is that schools are usually the one place that these children attend every day, where they can learn to have meaningful relationships and deal with their emotions. It is great when we can access the appropriate help from outside agencies. But we need to ensure we are doing as much as we can in school as well. If we are prepared to broaden our range of teaching strategies and expand our ways of thinking about these pupils, we can feel that we really have tried everything.

Of course, you might be thinking, why should we do this? Haven't we got enough to do already as teachers, without having to take on more new ideas? Isn't there already enough to do in a teaching day, without spending even more time worrying about these very challenging pupils?

The point is that we need to find ways to make our jobs easier and not more difficult. Very few of us feel satisfaction when a pupil is permanently excluded or stops coming to school. We are often left with a sense of weary dissatisfaction and uneasiness. If we can find ways of thinking which might give us a greater sense of satisfaction in our dealings with these pupils, surely they are worth a try.

In a workshop recently, Jason, an art teacher, said:

"I thought this was going to be just another workshop telling me that it was all my fault and I needed to work harder to engage certain pupils. Let's face it, that's all we are ever told, we need to find a new way of 'relating', a new 'approach'. As if we haven't got enough to do.

What I realised was that I often put my energies in the wrong direction, working harder and harder, but only trying variations of the same things, things which did not work. Realising it was not all about being competent in behaviour management, and by changing my way of thinking a bit, it actually made my teaching a bit easier and I felt better about myself as a teacher."

WHY THE PRINCIPLES UNDERPINNING BEHAVIOUR MANAGEMENT STRATEGIES DON'T HOLD TRUE FOR EVERY CHILD

Some of the assumptions and principles of behaviour management programmes don't match the internal and external worlds of these 'unteachable' children and young people. *Their life experience may have taught them not to trust relationships: behaviour management strategies inherently rely on the pupil trusting that the teacher has good intentions. They may have learned behaviours which serve a legitimate purpose in their everyday lives, but which are inappropriate and disruptive in schools.*

I will now look at some of the assumptions, and possible 'mismatches' between a model of the world which underpins a lot of classroom management practices, and the world as experienced by pupils from a background of trauma, neglect, loss and abuse. Later chapters will expand further on some of these ideas.

ASSUMPTION 1 POSITIVE ATTENTION LEADS TO BETTER BEHAVIOUR

Many behaviour management theories work on the assumption that rewarding appropriate behaviour and sanctioning inappropriate behaviour will lead children to learn better behaviour. There are some children for whom this is not the case. Life experience will have taught them a very different lesson, that positive attention cannot be trusted. They will find it very hard to accept positive feedback, or to make use of it to modify their behaviour.

Sally's sabotage (Part 1)

Eleven year old Sally was considered at risk of exclusion. She had been assigned a behaviour mentor to work with her and to try to engage her positively. The behaviour mentor took a lot of time to find out Sally's interests, and was able to include her in small group work on art and drama. Sally initially responded well and seemed to calm down with the individual, positive attention. However, after a few weeks, she started to say that she did not want to work with the mentor, and that she was 'stupid' and 'too old'. The mentor was upset but tried not to take it personally. She wondered if it was because she was now working with other girls in Sally's class.

One day Sally made an accusation against the mentor. She said that the mentor had got angry with her and pulled her out of a room. The school felt obliged to investigate the accusation, even though it was felt to be very unlikely. The mentor was understandably upset and other staff were very angry about the accusation, saying that it showed Sally did not deserve the extra attention and effort.

Although Sally subsequently withdrew the allegation, the mentor felt she could not work with Sally individually any more, and much of Sally's previous behaviour returned. It seemed that Sally was not able to make use of the positive, personal attention, and was too out-of-control to be managed in this way.

Hard as this was, it was necessary for the staff working with Sally to sit down and reflect on what had happened so that they could continue to work with her. What experience had Sally ever had of this type of personal interest and positive attention? Her early childhood was marked by abusive relationships and neglect. She had little experience of developing a trusting relationship with an adult. Perhaps this is why she had to sabotage it - it felt too dangerous to allow someone close. It was precisely because the mentor was getting through her barriers, that she had, at some level, to reject her. *(This case is discussed in more depth in Chapter 6 when I shall look at what might have been going on an unconscious level for Sally, and what was done subsequently to help her settle to learn)*

ASSUMPTION 2 CHOICE IS A GOOD THING

Many of the ideas in the preceding chapter rely on the idea that choice is a good thing, and we should build it into our behaviour management. Many of the strategies also rely on the inherent concept that if we give a child responsibility and discuss their rights and the likely consequences of each option, they will make good choices, behave better and be able to learn.

Life experience has taught some children and young people a very different lesson. They have learnt that they have no control over their own circumstances or their family's. They cannot perceive themselves as individuals who can make a choice, even a simple choice, and certainly not over important issues. They have rarely had experience of an adult asking their opinion or taking their wishes into account. When we attempt to do this, however respectfully, they may react in different ways - becoming compliant and passive or aggressive and argumentative, acting in or acting out. They will not therefore respond to basic boundaries in school in the way we expect.

Other children come from such chaotic situations of abuse and violence that they literally have no space in their brain to think about learning. As Barrett states (1991):

> In a classroom a teacher seems inaccessible to them; they are too anxious to make any use of skills to attract her attention ... These children cannot pay enough attention to feel able to make choices. (p. 24)

ASSUMPTION 3 DEVELOPMENTAL STAGES ARE REACHED BY A CERTAIN AGE

We tend to assume that children reach specific emotional and social developmental stages related to their chronological age. Secondary schools in particular are set up on the assumption that children have negotiated these life stages successfully, for example that they -

→ can take turns in a group
→ can show a teacher that they are listening without interrupting with their own stories
→ can wait for attention
→ are able to accept help willingly and do not expect ridicule or denigration for needing help
→ can explain their wants and needs in a socially acceptable way
→ are able to manage and express their emotions in an acceptable way most of the time
→ have a respect for other people's personal space

We will have pupils in our classes who have not achieved these developmental goals. In my work in secondary schools, I have often come across young people who are fourteen, and indeed look eighteen, but have some of the coping behaviours of a toddler.

Children who have not perhaps had the best start in life, or who are still living in very difficult circumstances, may not have had opportunities to learn these fundamental skills. In fact, their relationships with adults may have taught them another opposing set of skills. They may have learnt, for example, that they *will* be ridiculed if they ask for help, that their turn will *not* come if they wait politely, that their needs will not be met *unless* they express them angrily and defiantly.

ASSUMPTION 4 REPEATED EXAMPLES OF SUCCESS AND APPROPRIATE BEHAVIOUR WILL LEAD TO POSITIVE CHANGE

We tend to assume that if a child experiences success in a particular area, he or she will want to build up more of these kinds of experiences. This is indeed true for most children and young people. However, success may be something unknown and even feel dangerous to some of these 'unteachable' pupils. They will often have experienced only negative reinforcement, and that is the pattern they are used to. Strange as it may seem, it is negative feedback that makes them feel comfortable.

So in class, these children may seem to be enjoying some small successes. But then, seemingly out-of-the-blue, there might be a setback, which quickly escalates into a major incident. Despite the previous success, for example, keeping to their behaviour targets for a week or so, the child's behaviour seems worse than ever, and they seem totally unable to build on their small successes.

Perhaps we should not be surprised. Why should they believe in their fragile success, if it is burdened with needing to replace years of another type of conditioning?

If we are not careful, the tendency at this point is to throw up our hands and say we can do no more with these children and young people. It is, however, precisely at this point that there is a critical learning opportunity. If we can work with a young person to understand why things have gone wrong and how to move on from that, we can show them that mistakes are okay, that they will not be rejected for being imperfect. After all, how did we learn to walk? We fell over a lot, and someone encouraged us to get up and try again. If at some stage in our early life someone had told us not to get up until we could walk, we would never have learned to do so. In order to help young people change their behaviour, we need to understand and remember how real learning and change actually takes place. I have found the Motivational Cycle of Change (DiClemente & Prochaska 1994) to be a useful way of understanding this process, and how it applies to pupils trying to change their behaviour.

MOTIVATIONAL CYCLE OF CHANGE

If we take a moment to think what is involved in changing a behaviour, we can begin to understand why it is a complex process and not linear.

PAUSE FOR THOUGHT

Think about something you have tried to change about yourself, a target you set which you haven't reached

For example, losing weight, getting fit, giving up smoking - the usual type of New Year's Resolution!

Why did you give up or not succeed?

Generally there are reasons such as -

→ you, yourself, did not want the change badly enough; the motivation came from someone else or something external (for example, your doctor told you what you should be doing)
→ you did not really have a clear image of yourself making the change: you were not sure if was really you. I know, for example, that I find it difficult to keep going to a gym because I think that would make me a very boring person! That probably isn't true, but it's my own very limiting belief
→ the goal was too big to know where to start
→ the goal was too small to be motivating
→ there was a positive benefit in not changing. For example, many smokers I know believe they will be more stressed out if they give up smoking and there is a positive benefit in staying calm. Others almost unconsciously associate it with being a rebel and having fun, and are not convinced they can have that image of themselves as a non-smoker
→ other people did not support you or even sabotaged you. Have you noticed that if you are dieting, there is always someone who wants you to have a big piece of cake?

If we apply the above to thinking about why children and young people might have difficulty changing their behaviour in our schools, we can see that many of these elements may be inhibiting our pupils as well. Additionally,

→ there are benefits to getting angry: it can be quite cathartic, and keeping calm may not provide the same kind of release
→ the change may seem very big and not in keeping with their sense of self

→ they may not be noticed any more when they behave well: negative attention may be better than none at all
→ other people, such as their peer group, may start rejecting them or trying to make them go back to their old ways
→ they do not have an image of themselves as a 'good' student. In fact many say they do not want to be the 'swot' at the front with no friends, their image of the 'good' student
→ they see nothing to gain in changing. Other people are telling them they need to change, but it is not internally driven

Whilst children and young people may not be aware of all these factors, such issues may underlie the difficulty of trying to change habits - which is what their poor behaviour has become - and as such, are worthy of our consideration.

In the Motivational Cycle of Change, Prochaska & DiClemente (1994) identify the following stages in making and maintaining changes:

Pre-contemplation - the stage when we do not think there is a problem, even if other people are telling us otherwise
Contemplation - we begin to think we might need or want to change. We begin to consider the pros and cons of making the change
Determination/Planning - we decide we want to change, and make a plan about how to go about it
Action - we start carrying out our plan and making the change
Maintenance - we have managed to carry out the plan and demonstrate the change over time
Relapse - something goes wrong and we slip up, go back to our old ways. This slip-up can be triggered by an event or happen for no apparent reason
Exit - we have made the change and it has become part of the way we do things without us consciously realising

The important part of this model in relation to children changing their behaviour is that relapse is considered inevitable. In many different spheres of life, the most effective work on change takes this inevitability into account, and uses it as a key learning tool. For example, weight management programmes, which offer weekly 'weigh-ins', tell you to come back especially on the week you put on weight, as that is where the real learning takes place and that is where most people give up.

It is the same for the pupils who struggle to make behaviour changes. They will have developed their patterns of behaviour for good reasons. These patterns may have served children and young people well as a protection, and they will need to believe that this crucial function can be maintained in any change. They will relapse. This needs to be seen as a good thing, providing an opportunity to look at what needs to be built in to succeed another time. Unfortunately, it is the stage when many staff give up and say they have tried everything and can do no more with these children and young people.

ASSUMPTION 5 WE OUGHT TO BE ABLE TO BE IN CONTROL ALL THE TIME

We like to be in control. If we are honest, we are used to managing classes and groups successfully, and feeling that we have some control over what we are doing. Things happen both inside and outside school which are beyond our control. How we manage these times may affect how we feel and act on any given day. In most schools we probably have too much to do. The pressure to keep all the plates spinning can be immense, and if we are not careful, it can overwhelm us. On the days when certain children seem out-of-control, their behaviour can frustrate and enrage us, making it hard for us to hold on to our thinking.

ASSUMPTION 6 IF WE ARE PERFECT, THINGS WILL GO TO PLAN

Schools are full of people. We manage ourselves and relationships all day. Things happen which we cannot plan for because that is the nature of the human being. There is rarely a place to hide in a school day. I used to work in a bank and to be honest, there were days when I could hide behind paperwork, or plan my interactions to suit myself. We rarely have this opportunity in school. This is why there cannot be a linear relationship between what happens and how we deal with it. Things happen outside which affect how we feel and how we deal with challenging children. As teachers, therefore, we need to learn to be kinder to ourselves and to allow ourselves to be less than perfect. In fact, in the same way that Winnicott (1971) talks about 'good-enough mothering' being a key aspect in the early development of a child, we need to realise that it is possible to be a 'good-enough' teacher (*see* Chapter 8 *for more on Winnicott.*)

In the following chapters, I will look at managing these difficult relationships and working with children and young people from perspectives drawn from the world of therapy. These 'unteachable' pupils may not have had the best start in life, or may be now living in very difficult circumstances. I fundamentally believe that change is still possible for the great majority of them, and that teachers have a key role to play in this. If we can understand that change is not always as simple as we might wish, and allow ourselves to think about these children and ourselves in slightly different ways, we may find new possibilities for dealing with very challenging situations.

The next chapter will look at how ideas from psycho-analytic theory can give us extra insight.

In summary

Even the best and most experienced teachers will have problems dealing with pupils who have experienced poor starts in life. These children may have experienced trauma, neglect, loss, abuse and violence. There are therefore plentiful reasons why 'good' behaviour management strategies do not always work with these children.

- The underlying premises of most behaviour management programmes are alien to these children who have not had experience of a safe, logical world. In particular, they find it hard to
  - accept and trust positive attention and rewards
  - make and trust their own choices, and believe that they have permission to do so
  - choose without feeling they will be criticised for making a wrong choice
  - accept and trust the relationship with the teacher

- Some children are at different emotional and psychological developmental stages from those we might expect, given their chronological age. We need to be aware of this and work at the appropriate developmental stage

- The Motivational Cycle of Change can help us to understand why

(continues ...)

behaviour change is so difficult for all of us, but particularly these vulnerable children

- Relapse is an important part of change. Adults often give up at the point when they should persevere and help the child learn from the relapse

- We often unwittingly set targets in school for pupils for which they have no previous reference experience. For example, we might set a target of being able to ask for help: this assumes they have experience of an adult helping them without ridicule. Some children and young people may never have had this experience

- Relationship management is a key part of teaching. This is not always easy, as we are only human and cannot predict how we will react at every moment of the day

- We like to feel in control. These children make us feel as if we are losing control and we do not like that feeling. We sometimes overcompensate by trying to take control of things we cannot control at that time

- Children without boundaries go in search of them. They will not automatically accept boundaries if they have never experienced them, but this does not mean they do not need them

Chapter 4

But I'm not a therapist, I'm a teacher!

WHY DO WE NEED TO LEARN ABOUT IDEAS FROM THERAPY?

In the workshops I run for teachers, participants often say, "*All this sounds fine in theory, but what has it got to do with teaching?*"

It's a fair question, and in this chapter I will explain how an understanding of ideas from therapy can give us some extra insight for teaching these children and young people. I will also outline some of the perceived obstacles to using therapeutic thinking in the classroom, and then suggest some of the advantages.

Most teachers I have met and worked with would agree that they would indeed like more understanding of the children and young people I've described. However, the 'answer' to the challenges they present often seems to be to get specialist help. Schools hope that by organising a referral to an outside agency, such as a counselling service or CAMHS, they have done the right thing, and the child will get the appropriate kind of help which cannot be provided in school.

Indeed, some children are lucky and can engage with these specialist services. However, in my experience of working with children at risk of exclusion - both as a teacher and a therapist - I've found that waiting lists in clinics are often extensive. In addition, even when a child gets an appointment, it cannot be certain that the child and family will engage with an outside service. Quite often they find it difficult to attend the clinic and appointments are missed.

Dan's lack of trust

Dan was fourteen. He had been diagnosed with ADHD at a young age and was on medication. He was referred to my unit as he was considered to be academically gifted but underperforming due to his challenging behaviour and poor work rate. He saw a psychiatrist once a month for his medication. He often refused to go and said his mother could just pick up repeat prescriptions. After I discussed the situation with him, he asked me to come with him to CAMHS to see "why no-one listens to that old bloke".

In the meeting, the psychiatrist made some very pertinent points which, I later pointed out to Dan, we had also discussed at school. He said "Yeah, but why listen to him? You know me 'cos you see me every day here". Dan also told me that he did not think he had ADHD but that his mother would lose some money if he stopped taking the tablets, so he just "went along with it".

Dan was an example of a child who DID have access to specialist help, but he saw help in school as more relevant and somehow easier to accept. His safe relationship was with staff at the school and those were the people he trusted. He was playing a kind of game with the clinic, in order to keep his mum happy. He was not allowing them to work with him in any deeper way.

Dan needed the staff at school to reinforce the messages from the psychiatrist - primarily that he was a good person and knew how to be kind, so did not need to get attention by being unkind. After some liaison with the clinic, I was able to ask staff to promote this message with Dan and to use these exact words. In time, Dan learned that he could get attention in better ways at school and that people in school were prepared to see a better, kinder side to him. He was able to finish his GCSEs and get a training place at college.

As an educational psychotherapist, I have also worked with younger pupils in the CAMHS clinic myself who could not attend regularly because their parents found it very difficult to keep appointments. I often felt frustrated, thinking that if I were in school, I would have more immediate access to these children. It might not offer what Bomber (2007) refers to as '*the protected space of the therapy room*' (p.47), but the more public space of the classroom might be the best chance these children get in which to experience safe, consistent relationships.

James' non-attendance

James was a seven year old boy referred to CAMHS due to an escalation of violent and aggressive behaviour at home. He was particularly aggressive to his younger brother. The family had been involved with CAMHS before but had never attended regularly. This time the parents had agreed to see a Family Therapist whilst I worked with James on an individual basis.

The first four weeks were fine, attendance was good and James engaged well with the work. I learned that he liked school and was doing well. His mother reported that things were calmer at home. In the fifth week, however, he did not attend. His mother called to say that their car had broken down. They did not attend the following week either.

I discussed this with the Family Therapist, who said there had been some difficult issues in the parents' last session with her. We managed to get James to come in a couple more times, but there was a pattern of non-attendance when things seemed to improve and then attendance after a crisis. Eventually, the family stopped attending.

This was a case which, as a teacher, I would have thought was going well, as we had got the CAMHS referral and the services required. However, in the clinic, there were limits to the work we could do, due to the child's non-attendance (since his attendance was dependent on an adult bringing him). It would have been James' teachers who saw the child most regularly and who were, apart from his parents, the most influential adults in his life.

If I had been teaching James in school, I would have able to see him more often. This would have allowed me to maintain the relationship and work with him without being reliant on his parents' attendance. If, as a teacher, I also had some understanding of the approach of the therapist, I might have been in a better position to be help him process his feelings and anxieties.

However, the two disciplines of teaching and therapy are often viewed as completely separate fields. As a participant at a workshop recently commented,

> *"But I'm not a therapist, I'm a teacher. I don't have the time or the training to psycho-analyse these pupils and their problems. I just want to teach them what's on my scheme of work."*

This, of course, is true, teachers do not need to be therapists or vice versa. We can, however, use some of the ideas from the field of therapy in order to gain a greater understanding of our difficult-to-reach pupils and then to devise more effective ways of teaching them. I will now look at how connections can be made between the two in order to help us teach vulnerable and challenging pupils.

THE USEFUL CONNECTIONS BETWEEN TEACHING AND THERAPY

Having trained as a secondary teacher and then as an educational psychotherapist, I can see value in both ways of working. Moreover, the two roles are not necessarily mutually exclusive. I am particularly interested in how ideas from therapeutic thinking can help teachers work with challenging pupils and in effect, make life in the classroom a little easier for everyone. Spending time thinking around therapeutic ideas has helped me greatly in my own work with challenging young people. It has also helped the staff who worked with me. Libby, a Behaviour Support Assistant:

> *"Sometimes I used to despair about my knowledge and ability when dealing with certain children. I always felt there must be something more I could be doing. When I learned a bit about attachment theory, I began to see their behaviour in a different light, I could think about their needs and what their behaviour was showing me about them. It didn't give me any miracle cures, but it did give me food for thought and helped me consider some other strategies."*

Teaching can be a hard job. Any book you take the time to read should make your life a bit easier (or a lot!) and above all, help you engage more pupils in learning. My main aim in writing this book is to provide you with additional frameworks for thinking about these seemingly unteachable children and young people, by connecting up the best ideas from therapy and teaching.

WHAT HAPPENS WHEN WE THINK OF BRINGING IDEAS FROM THERAPY INTO SCHOOLS?

In my experience, the word 'therapy' can provoke mixed reactions in teachers. I have often heard *"Well, I am not a therapist"* or *"He/she needs specialist therapy"* in response to some of my suggestions for dealing with a particular pupil. I realised that some of the ideas seemed to evoke wariness and mistrust, particularly those that sounded a bit too much like 'psycho-babble' (such as thinking about unconscious processes). When I was running an on-site unit for pupils at risk of exclusion, it seemed that even the more pro-active teachers were unsure about trying out some of the ideas. They would say the suggestions were interesting, but not relevant to a class of thirty pupils.

I began to wonder why thinking about behaviour in a different way seems so difficult at times in school. Perhaps it is the lack of shared knowledge about each profession which leads to unhelpful assumptions about what each entails and values.

I have to admit that I probably had ambivalent feelings about therapy myself. When I began training to be a therapist, I thought the ideas were great for working with pupils, but I remained reluctant to start my own personal therapy. If I am honest, I thought therapy was for 'fixing' what was broken. I was not broken and didn't need 'fixing'! When I did eventually go to a psychotherapist (as part of the training requirement), I sat in silence for most of the first session to 'prove' I did not have to talk first. However, I gradually came to realise that, although I would readily advise others of the benefits of counselling or therapy, I was finding it difficult to look at myself in this way. It took me some while to allow myself to get involved, but when I did, I came to appreciate the value of having a reflective space to think and to get a different perspective on everyday problems. It was a worthwhile, albeit extremely challenging, experience.

I wonder if many other teachers feel the same way about therapy - in principle a good thing, but not really for them, not for those who work in the 'real' world of timetables, targets and challenging children.

So what I am going to do is to look at the common perception of the differences between teaching and therapy, in order to see which aspects can be applied to the classroom and which parts may need to stay in the therapy room.

PUTTING THE DIVIDE BETWEEN THERAPY AND TEACHING IN PERSPECTIVE

I feel it is useful to begin by thinking about the differences between therapy and teaching. Groups of staff that I have worked with over the years - both teaching and non-teaching staff - come up with remarkably similar lists. These lists usually include:

TEACHING	THERAPY
Teacher-centred	Client-centred
Imposed curriculum	Topic comes from client
Public	Private
Group	1-to-1
Subject-focused	Emotions can be the focus
Talking	Listening
Accountable to others	Accountable to the client
Short on time	Have time to think
Not paid for by client	Usually paid for by client
Poor behaviour unhelpful	Poor behaviour can be helpful
Teacher knows	Client knows
Teacher has power	Client has power
Teacher makes choices	Client makes choices

...and you might like to add your own.

Looking at the two lists, it seems that many of the items on the therapy side could be relevant to the classroom situation. Most teachers I have spoken to would be striving for child-centred classes and schools, which allow time for thinking to develop. Most would like to think they listen to their pupils and are aware of emotional factors which influence learning. Most teachers would like to think that they are encouraging their pupils to feel empowered, and able to make good choices.

Moreover, we could also challenge some of the apparent restrictions and limits to using a therapeutic approach. The one I hear most is that teachers do not have enough time to work in this way. Many teachers tell me they would like to know more about therapeutic approaches but that they do not have the time in the packed curriculum. Indeed, when I undertook a placement as an educational psychotherapist in a CAMHS clinic, the first thing I noticed was that it was very quiet, and I had a lot of built-in time to think and reflect on my cases. It made me realise how rarely there seemed to be time to do this in school. However, the experience convinced me that we can make time in schools. Indeed we need to make time. We make time for other things we believe are important and which will have an impact on our teaching and learning. In my view, making time for reflection and thinking about behaviour in a pro-active and not purely reactive way needs to be given a similar priority. Taking the time to do this is not a waste of time. It ought to save us time eventually, if it leads to more effective solutions.

I hope that by taking the time to read this book, you will realise that there are ways we can build some of the ideas from educational psychotherapy into our classroom teaching. For example, in the next chapter, I shall look at the idea of projection and how we often have feelings projected onto us by the children in our class. How long would it take to reflect on the emotion or feeling being projected onto you by a young person, plus a moment to name it or re-frame it? (*see* p.156) Is this any longer than it takes to end up in a damaging confrontation? How long does it take to remember which football team a pupil supports and show, by offering him or her a quick comment, that they are being as Bion, (1961, 1970) would say, 'held in mind'? (*and see* p.124). It is perhaps our perception of how long integrating new ideas will take that is the issue.

Teachers also often tell me that they are worried about talking about emotions and feelings, fearing they might open a 'Pandora's Box' - in other words, elicit information and issues which they do not know how to handle in their classroom. This is of course a valid point, and it is only right that we are aware of the influence our words and actions can have. I am not suggesting that all teachers should now rush off and start working as therapists with a class of thirty! That could be dangerous. However, the feelings and emotions are already present in our classrooms and are being shown to us all the time. They are being demonstrated to us by the way certain pupils behave and, they are an integral part of what happens in the relationships between children and teachers. By gaining an understanding of what is happening between us and the young people in our classrooms, we may find another way to manage these relationships and critical incidents - or at least to manage our own feelings about them and thus give ourselves - and perhaps our pupils - an easier time.

While I believe it is possible to integrate some ideas from the therapy world into teaching, I am aware that there are factors which make it difficult to implement appropriate strategies and to hold onto a therapeutic way of thinking in the classroom. I will now consider why it can be difficult to maintain some of these ideas in schools today.

SO WHY IS IT DIFFICULT TO INTEGRATE IDEAS FROM THERAPY INTO TEACHING?

What these pupils seem to 'do to us'

Most of us will acknowledge that it can be difficult to reflect on the meaning of some children's challenging behaviour in our classes. The behaviours stir up strong feelings, both at a conscious and unconscious level, in those of us trying to deal with them. When we are overwhelmed by these kind of strong feelings, it can be very difficult to think clearly. Our thought processes are hijacked by our emotions.

Sue Panter has written that:

> It must be recognised that the area of pupil behaviour is highly emotive. It challenges teachers' sense of their own professional competence and both teachers' and parents' self-esteem … emotions often get in the way of constructive planning. (Gray & Panter, 2000, p.7)

And indeed, it is often the case that everyone feels as if they are failing and that their competence is being challenged. Parents feel that they are failing, as they 'should' be able to bring up children who behave appropriately in school. Such an overwhelming feeling of failure is very hard to tolerate and may lead to the unconscious need to project it onto someone else - often the teacher or key adult dealing with their child (*see* Chapter 6 *for more on projection*). So the parents very often come in and shout at school staff, telling us that we 'should' know what to do with their children in the classroom. Teachers feel that they are failing so they, in turn, feel angry and rail against the system, the curriculum, other agencies, the child and the child's family. The pupil in the middle of all this knows they are failing, so they shout at everyone, or 'shout' through other kinds of disruptive behaviour

Faced with such overwhelming feelings of failure, it can be easier, or at least less uncomfortable, to avoid thinking about these feelings and become distracted into discussing who we should refer these pupils to. I have sat in many multi-agency meetings where we have all tried our best to come up with solutions for these hard-to-reach children, but have often ended up defending our own organisation or actions and wondering why other agencies cannot attend or play their part. Perhaps we need to acknowledge at these meetings that it is painful to accept the feelings of inadequacy that these children evoke in all of us. This can free us up to discuss the real issues, without getting caught up in a cycle of blame. If we acknowledge our own difficulties and vulnerability, we can share ideas and accept help from each other without feeling incompetent and defensive.

Accepting help does not mean you are incompetent. Offering help does not mean you think someone else is incompetent. But this is what it sometimes feels like. Why is that?

Pressures on teachers - why is everything 'our fault'?

Sometimes, if you read the papers, it can seem as if schools and education are responsible for everything. Failing schools are named and shamed. Stories which make the headlines are those which feature pupils rioting or out-of-control.

Gill, the Head of a large secondary school says;

> *"Last week I spent most of my time trying to prevent a story appearing in the local press about an incident involving a fight in school. Somehow the editor of the paper had got wind of it. The whole thing had been blown out of proportion and I had sleepless nights, imagining headlines such as 'school out-of-control'. In the same week, our GCSE drama group performed brilliantly at a national conference on domestic violence but no-one was interested in printing that."*

Far less is reported about the everyday life of a challenging school, where there is a huge amount of excellent work going on, and daily, many small but important successes. There is pressure from the government, from Ofsted, from managers, from parents and there are also pressures which come from ourselves. We need to be able to work together and learn from each other in order to maintain a balanced perspective.

PAUSE FOR THOUGHT

Take a few minutes and think about all the things you are worried about at the moment, particularly things which may affect your ability to consider new ideas and the processes behind challenging behaviour

Now make two lists - those things you can change and those you can't. Add a rough figure for how much of your time you find yourself thinking about each item - once or twice a week, for example, or several times a day?

Notice how much of our time is spent on those things over which we have no real control at the moment. This is how we can put pressure on ourselves. We spend time focusing on the things we cannot change. We cannot MAKE these children change their behaviour. We can be curious about what is driving it and help them to think about it with us.

An example of a teacher's own pressure inhibiting creative thinking

I was speaking to a teacher about playing music in his classes. He said he liked to play calming music when the students were occupied in a task. He thought it had a good effect on the atmosphere and relationship in class. He said he did not think he would do it in the forthcoming Ofsted inspection as "they might not like it".

I was astounded. I said there was a lot of evidence that music was a good idea and asked him why he felt he could not follow his beliefs. He smiled and said "I think I am just one of those people who plays it safe, Marie."

What a pity! The Head of the school thought very highly of this teacher. He was certainly not going to change his mind after Ofsted but this teacher was putting himself under pressure to 'perform' for the inspectors, leaving him unable to pay attention to what he knew worked.

Far too little attention is paid to teachers' own emotions and feelings. There is now an emphasis on introducing SEAL in primary and secondary schools in the UK, which is definitely a step in the right direction. But how much time is given to teachers to explore their own feelings and reactions to the pressures of the day, or to explore what is happening on an unconscious and conscious level between them and their students? In my experience as a teacher, there is hardly any time put aside for this. When working as a psychotherapist, it is an accepted part of the supervision process.

WHY SHOULD IT BE LEFT TO TEACHERS TO TACKLE THESE ISSUES?

Mark is a very pro-active Headteacher. He is totally committed to the idea that the children in his school need to work on their emotional development in order to be in a state of readiness to learn. He admits 'off-the-record' and looking very guilty, that part of him deep down is angry that schools are having to provide all of this instead of other government agencies, which he feels are better placed to deal with it.

Like Mark, I agree that other agencies and professionals need to be involved with these children and their families: teachers cannot solve the problems on their own. However, schools are still the places where these children come most days, and teachers are the adults who interact with them most often outside the home. We, as teachers, are therefore best placed to deal with some of the issues on the spot and to see the daily patterns of interaction. So we need to be prepared to accept that our job is to help children and young people develop emotional and mental states for learning, as well as help them to acquire specific subject knowledge. This is perhaps one of the greatest challenges in teaching, but can also be one of the most rewarding.

WHAT 'BITS' OF THEORY CAN BE USEFUL THEN?

Although teachers do not need to become therapists, an understanding of unconscious mental processing and psycho-dynamic concepts could help staff understand and deal with the feelings and behaviour inherent in the relationships with 'unteachable' pupils. In the following chapters, I will look in more detail at the theories and concepts which I have found most useful in my own teaching:

1. Unconscious psychological defence mechanisms (Chapter 6)
2. Attachment Theory (Chapter 7)
3. Bion's theory of containment (Chapter 7)
4. Winnicott's theories on play (Chapter 8)
5. How pupils' experiences of loss affect their ability to cope with beginnings, transitions and endings (Chapter 9)

In summary

- There has traditionally been a divide between how teachers work and how therapists work. Working with these 'unteachable' children is often seen as the work of a specialist outside school
- It is not always possible to access the right sort of help outside school and in isolation it is also not necessarily enough
- School is the place where children learn most about relationships and themselves in relation to others

- You do not need to be a therapist to apply some therapeutic thinking to a situation

- Some common ideas about therapy which could be incorporated into our thinking about teaching are that:
  - It could be client (student) -centred
  - The topic could come from the student
  - We can have private discussions
  - We can make time for 1-to-1 discussions
  - Emotions can be the focus
  - We can develop our listening skills
  - We can see ourselves as more accountable to the client (student)
  - We could make more space and time to think
  - Poor behaviour could be seen as a helpful indicator of what the student needs
  - We can trust that the student knows things that we do not
  - We could allow the student some power over the interaction
  - We could allow the student to make choices

  It should be possible to integrate these elements into our teaching approach

- Admitting to our own feelings and emotions is part of the process

- These children's behaviour can create 'attacks on thinking', leaving us unable to think creatively about solutions. Such paralysis in the thinking of the adults around these children can lead to frustration and blaming

(continues ...)

- There are many pressures on teachers which sometimes limit our capacity to think creatively and take risks. We need to acknowledge which pressures are real and which are ones we have created ourselves
- It does not take a lot of time to use this approach. It involves a shift in thinking
- We all need to be prepared to learn from other agencies and professions in our approach
- Part of our role is to recognise, acknowledge and manage feelings - our pupils' and our own. Time needs to be built in to allow this to happen, in the same way that it happens in other professions such as psychotherapy

Chapter 5

What is happening with these children and young people?

> A child's current behaviour often reflects an essentially sane response to an untenable set of life circumstances.
>
> (Bray 1997, *quoted in* Visser & Rayner, 1999, p.79)

We have looked at some of the issues for teachers. Now let's turn to the issues preventing these students from being able to learn.

What do children and young people need to be able to do in order to learn? Any description of a good learner tends to include the following characteristics and skills:

→ feels safe and is willing to take risks
→ has good self-esteem
→ can seek help when needed without expecting criticism or ridicule
→ is able to concentrate and ignore distractions
→ is able to manage frustration, anxiety and disappointment
→ has the capacity to bear not knowing
→ is optimistic and has a positive attitude to a problem
→ can wait for attention.

Through consistency of care, a child acquires the sense of safety and security he needs to pass through the developmental stages mentioned on p.36. A parent or carer does not have to be perfect, but needs to provide what Winnicott (1962) calls 'good-enough' care. This means being able to attune to the child's basic needs for the majority of time.

By passing through the milestones, a child usually acquires many of the characteristics of a good learner mentioned above. For example, the child learns that if his parent or carer cannot attend to his needs immediately, she will not forget him and will come back soon. If the child is upset, he will learn that the parent or carer will try to understand his distress and provide comfort. If the child makes a mistake, the parent or carer will encourage him to try again, and praise his efforts. If a child has not had this kind of experience in his early years, it will impact on his later learning and ability to benefit from other relationships in the classroom.

Fundamentally, in order to learn, a child or young person needs to feel safe enough to accept the powerlessness and frustration of not knowing something. Learning takes place at that point where we struggle to match what we know with what seems to be new and different. Those whose internal and external worlds are dangerous may not be able to take this risk. When we consider some of the young people in our classes, we can see that they have often not had the opportunity to experience situations in which to acquire the necessary skills and characteristics. In fact, for many, the opposite has happened.

Let's imagine ourselves in their place. If we feel unsafe, bad about ourselves and have only experienced ridicule and pain when seeking help, we are not going to be able to act in a positive way in a classroom. If we have a parent who cannot give us adequate attention, or if we have had to fight with our siblings to get any attention at all, it might feel unbearable to have to wait even for a second for the teacher to come over. If we have lived in constant turmoil and fear, we need to be hyper-vigilant. We won't be able to focus on a task in the classroom, for fear of not noticing something dangerous coming from the environment or from the other children or adults there. These kind of thoughts may lead us - usually unconsciously - to want to defend ourselves from hurt and disappointment. (*See* Chapter 6 *for more on the defence mechanisms which may be in operation in our classrooms*)

RISK FACTORS

Children who may be at risk of losing or never acquiring the capacity to learn can usually be identified by certain factors present in their early life or current circumstances. Examples of these risk factors are:

• Parental alcohol and drug-taking • Neglect •
• Parental mental health illness • Bereavements • Emotional Abuse •
• Physical abuse • Sexual abuse • Domestic violence •
• Loss, separations, complex family relationships •
• Several moves, involving continual changes of home and school •

Those children and young people whom we consider 'unteachable' often have multiple risk factors impacting on them and their ability to perform in school.

WHAT HAPPENS WHEN YOU HAVE LIVED IN A CHAOTIC, FEARFUL SITUATION WHERE 'GOOD-ENOUGH' CARE HAS NOT BEEN AVAILABLE?

If babies and young children experience a lack of 'attuned, sensitive care' they will have abnormally high levels of stress hormones, including cortisol, in their bodies. High levels of cortisol are known to significantly impair the growth and development of the baby's brain and body. High cortisol levels can therefore affect a child's ability to think, to retrieve information and to manage his or her own behaviour. Children who experience trauma and loss also seem to have significant parts of their brains not 'hooked up'. Connections between neurons in the part of the child's brain responsible for empathy, logic, cause and effect, and reasoning, have often been made inadequately. Because the brain has had to behave as if under constant fear of attack, the 'flight-and-fight' response triggered by the oldest part of the brain is over-used.

Research shows that the brain develops in a 'use-dependent' manner, and organises and re-organises itself in response to this (Shore 2002). This means that these children often operate as if they are in a constant state of fear and anxiety. Their brains will respond to any perceived threat by going into a flight, fright or freeze mode. We can see it in class when they seem to over-react to any perceived criticism, change of plan or challenging new work. They will be 'programmed' to respond in certain ways and this takes time and care to 're-programme'. So, it will be impossible to settle to learning in a classroom as their brains are on constant 'high-alert', unable to focus on the tasks, needing to be on the look-out for potential harm in the environment. *(For a more detailed description of the effects of high stress and cortisol in babies, see Gerhardt, 2004)*

WHAT ARE THE EFFECTS OF TRAUMA, LOSS AND NEGLECT ON CHILDREN?

All children react differently to their life circumstances, and there are many factors which help some children to be more resilient than others. There are, however, some common patterns of behaviour which we may notice in the classroom in children and young people who have experienced extreme situations such as trauma, loss, abuse and neglect. I will discuss these in more detail in the chapters on Attachment Theory and psychological defence mechanisms, but will mention some of the key issues briefly here to clarify why some children and young people cannot settle to learn in even the best planned lessons and most organised classrooms.

CHILDREN AND YOUNG PEOPLE AFFECTED BY DOMESTIC VIOLENCE

Natalie's anger

Natalie is a year 6 pupil. She is quite big for her age and other pupils are frightened of her. She is on the Child Protection register and there have been reports of domestic violence at home.

*Today she arrives late into class and glares at her classteacher, Ms Jenkins, muttering angrily, "This **** school, I hate it and I hate you." Ms Jenkins chooses to ignore this and smiles at Natalie, saying it is nice to see her and that there is a chair on the front table. Natalie scowls and says she won't sit there, she hates sitting there. Ms Jenkins can feel herself getting annoyed but struggles to stay calm. She says that Natalie needs to sit there for today so that she can continue her excellent work from yesterday. Natalie starts shouting and saying that it is not fair, Ms Jenkins is picking on her, never listens to her and her work from yesterday was rubbish anyway. Ms Jenkins eventually has had enough. She tells Natalie to sit down or she will have to be sent to the Head. Natalie storms out, saying she will go and tell the Head herself and that she is leaving this stupid school anyway.*

What could be happening with pupils like Natalie?

Pupils who have witnessed or been subjected to domestic violence at home will have experienced and will continue to experience a maelstrom of emotions and feelings. They may unconsciously re-create violent interactions with adults in school, as on some level, this is what their brains have become accustomed to. They may at times be aggressive, seeming to empathise with the aggressor in conflict situations, and may seem to despise what they see as weakness in others. Such an attitude may sometimes cause them to bully other weaker or 'different' children.

This can be very hard for staff in schools to understand, as we often have the idea that someone who has experienced such hurt would not do to others what they had suffered themselves. But children who have been in these situations may have been left with feelings of anger towards both parents, the victim for allowing the violence and the aggressor for causing it. They will have strong and conflicting emotions which cannot safely be expressed at home. They will not necessarily respond to well-meaning adults in school. Why should they trust praise and gentleness? This is not what their lives have conditioned them to understand or trust.

CHILDREN AND YOUNG PEOPLE AFFECTED BY LOSS

Brian can't accept help

Brian is a year 5 pupil who is in foster care. He has irregular contact with his birth mother and has not seen his father since he was two years old. Although he has been in his current foster placement for twelve months, he had a series of short-term placements in the preceding years when he went back and forth between his birth mother and foster carers.

Brian can sometimes behave well in school, but is reluctant to try new things or meet new people. There have been reports of him bullying younger children and demanding they hand over their lunch money. He is meant to have help from a Teaching Assistant, but he refuses to work with her and gets very angry when she tries to sit next to him.

Today he comes into school late. He walks around the corridors for some time, pretending to be looking for his class. He ignores a Teaching Assistant who comes out of a classroom to ask him if he needs help. Eventually, he is brought to class by the Deputy Head who has found him in the dining-room. He comes in, sits on his own and seems very busy, looking in his bag and taking out several coloured pens. A child at the front whispers to the teachers, Ms James, that the gold pen is hers. Ms James is unsure what to do, whether to acknowledge Brian's arrival or to tackle the issue of pens. She decides to greet him positively and ask the Teaching Assistant to work with him. He immediately says that he knows what to do (even though he was not there when it was explained) and he does not need any help. He takes out his favourite book and starts to write out words from it, something which he had already done yesterday.

What could be happening with children like Brian?

Many children in our classrooms have experienced loss and rejection of some kind. Some may have had multiple instances of loss in their lives. The loss may have been one or more bereavements, but can also include changes brought on by divorce, separation, family upheaval and continual moving of the family home.

Students who have experienced loss and rejection may become very controlling, not wanting to admit that they need anyone to help them learn. The urge to control may express itself in anger towards those trying to help, or in seeming indifference. Many of these children find change in schools very hard to cope with, as they associate it with people going away and sudden, unexplained loss. They may expect the worst, be unwilling to take the necessary risks to learn, or refuse to move onto new things. They may have unconscious underlying feelings of anger at a parent or loved one for leaving them, as well as sadness at the loss. These conflicting feelings can be particularly confusing if the parent has taken their own life, or died through an addiction. The child cannot learn because their own feelings are so mixed up and seem potentially dangerous. Some children may become school refusers as their excessive worry about a remaining parent/carer leads to a huge separation anxiety.

Others may find it difficult to enjoy success and positive experiences at school, as they are convinced it could be snatched away at any moment.

CHILDREN AND YOUNG PEOPLE AFFECTED BY ADDICTION

Jane's anxiety (Part 1)

Jane is a year 8 pupil who is driving her teachers to distraction. They know that there have been some problems at home; Jane is on the Child Protection Register as there were reports of drug dealing from her house. Today she has Maths first lesson with her Head of Year, Mr Marshall. In the previous Maths lesson Jane had completed all her work neatly and quickly. She had worked quietly, without comment, for the whole lesson.

Jane jumps up when Mr Marshall enters the room and offers to give out the books and write the date on the board. When he does not acknowledge her immediately - he is reading a note from another pupil - she gets up from her seat and starts writing on the board anyway. Mr Marshall thanks her and lets her give out the books, he knows that she likes to do jobs and to get praise for doing so. He then asks her to sit down and open her own book. She sits down but starts to ask him if he is going to the year 8 inter-form football match after school. He says he might and tries to focus her on the task.

As he starts the lesson, Mr Marshall takes care to come over and check that Jane knows what to do. Jane begins to ask him if she can come to help him at break. Mr Marshall says they can talk about this later and then is called over by another student who is having problems understanding the task. Jane watches him go, then starts calling loudly, "Sir, Sir I don't know what to do. Can you come and help me?" Mr Marshall says he will come back in a minute. Jane is quiet for a moment and then starts calling out again.

Mr Marshall - unusually for him - snaps, and says "Oh for heaven's sake, Jane, just wait your turn." Jane sulks for the rest of the lesson, and does no work (for more on Jane, see p.106).

What could be happening with pupils like Jane?

Children who have lived with a parent who is suffering from an addiction, such as drugs or alcohol, may not have experienced a consistent pattern of responses from the adult. They may have experienced times when the adult was very available to them and other times when their needs were not being met. These children may not respond well to consistency from school staff, as they do not trust it. They expect every day to be different, and will sometimes unconsciously provoke staff into behaving inconsistently. These students may have an unusually volatile range of highs and lows in their own moods. They will seem hard to teach, as we cannot predict their response from one day to the next. They will constantly seek to keep the attention of the teacher as they will not believe they will be remembered if the teacher's attention is on another pupil. For them, inconsistency and unpredictability is the norm.

CHILDREN AND YOUNG PEOPLE AFFECTED BY PARENTAL MENTAL ILLNESS

Raj's perfectionism

Raj is a year 9 pupil who always tries hard in class and listens quietly to the teacher. Today he has History with Ms Lambert. Ms Lambert likes Raj. She knows that his mother has been ill recently and was hospitalised with depression. He does not appear to want to talk about it.

Today he has not been able to complete his homework as he spent several hours at home trying to get it perfect. Each time he had almost finished, he found a mistake and ripped it up to start again. He is sitting at the front of the class trying to finish his most recent homework attempt. Ms Lambert is keen to acknowledge the effort Raj is making. She praises his work and tries to stop him ripping up work if he is not satisfied. Although he is not a problem to her, she has a niggling feeling that all is not well. He seems too focused on being perfect and can react extremely to small things, such as not being able to find a sharpener for his pencil.

What could be happening with pupils like Raj?

There will be some children in our classes who do not 'act out'. They may appear quiet and withdrawn, or indeed like the 'perfect' student. Children who have dealt with a parental mental illness can exhibit this kind of behaviour. They may consciously or unconsciously believe that they need to make sure they are not a burden, that their needs will not be too overwhelming for their parent to cope with.

In school, they can be controlling, wanting to keep everything in order, and unwilling to admit to problems. They may also be excessively anxious, but will not necessarily appear so. They may appear very calm, and then suddenly have eruptions of anger or crying over quite a small incident. In their world, they find it hard to distinguish between an ordinary sad feeling and a complete disaster, so they damp down those feelings until they 'leak' out. This can lead some young people in this group to self-harm. They have not experienced an adult who can 'contain' their feelings (- that is, who tries to understand, name and acknowledge the difficult feelings they are experiencing and who does not panic or over-react, thus helping them learn to manage their emotional experience (*see* p.124 *for more on containment*) and may therefore be unwilling to trust and let the adult teach them.

OTHER FACTORS WHICH MAY BE UNCONSCIOUSLY AFFECTING LEARNING AND CLASSROOM BEHAVIOUR

- *The sense that relationships can be dangerous*
  For some children, relationships can feel very threatening. We have seen that many of our strategies for managing behaviour rely on developing good relationships with pupils. If a child has not experienced a caring, consistent relationship with an adult, they will not be able to trust those offered by teachers in school.

- *Difficulties in focusing on the task*
  We can see that for many of these children, such as Jane and Natalie, there is a need to be hyper-vigilant and to check out the relationship with the teacher at all times. Children who have lived in volatile, violent, insecure circumstances where it was vital to gauge the mood of the adults in order to survive, may not be able to focus on classroom tasks. Their primary objective is to maintain and check out their relationship with the teacher. They have no space in their mind for the task.

- *The way targets are set in school*
  Many behaviour targets operate on the conditioned response and reward principle. If I set a seemingly achievable target with a child and monitor when they are doing it - the 'catch them being good' principle - theory suggests that they will learn to do more of the behaviour we want. That works with the majority of children who have had some experience of the kind of targets we are setting for them. In the case of these other 'unteachable' children, however, we are setting them targets for which they have no prior similar experience to refer to.

For example, we may give them the target of sitting still, focusing, and showing they can concentrate on their own work for ten minutes. How does a child know what it is like to be concentrating? What lets them know that they are doing this thing called 'focusing'? They are likely to have had very few experiences of this, either from a shared experience with a thinking adult or on their own in a calm environment. So how can they understand what we asking for, and how will they know if they are doing it? Knowing about something in theory and experiencing it in person are two different things. At some stage in our life, someone needs to put a name to these experiences so that we know what they are. As children, we need adults to help us make sense of our experience and name the experiences we are having.

- *The effect of different curricula*
  We are used to thinking about how to adapt the subject-related content of our curriculum for pupils in our class. It is useful to also bear in mind that the underlying concepts of particular subjects can pose a threat to the thinking of some children, and create confusion in their minds. Certain subjects may stir up unconscious anxieties and memories. A few examples are listed below.

History

History can be scary for children with disrupted and confusing backgrounds. I have worked with children who cannot keep track of the number of times they have moved or the times and dates of key events in their lives. They will find it equally hard to bear the thought of thinking back in time. The simple act of drawing up a timeline can seem overwhelming. They may act as if they cannot understand the concept at all. At some level, these children and young people may find it safer to stay in the 'here and now' than to allow their brains to accept the concept of past time.

Geography

Some aspects of Geography relate to people and places. For children who have no place or do not know where they belong, the study of populations, towns and countries where people have a sense of identity can seem nonsensical. They may consciously reject the subject by saying it is boring and pointless, or unconsciously by seeming not to be able to learn. Geography may stir up unwanted questions about where they come from. It may indeed stir up feelings of loss, of displacement of loved ones.

English

We often ask children to write about themselves in English. GCSE English requires you to write an autobiography. This can be too painful for some children. I have often dealt with young people in Year 10 who are causing disruption in class and not getting on with their work, only to realise the problems started with the seemingly simple task of writing an autobiography. For others, it is impossible to write about themselves because they have no sense of self.

On the other hand, English - if it is about other characters - can sometimes provide a vehicle through stories, plays and drama for these children to explore their feelings in a safe way.

Science

Some elements of the Science curriculum involve ordering, sorting and classifying items. It can be very hard to understand the concept of logic and order if you have not had much or any of this in your life's experience.

Jason's confusion

Jason was a Year 8 boy who seemed to enjoy Science experiments and discussing how things worked. However, he could not retain any information about categories of elements and food and so on. In fact each time it was presented he acted as if it was the first time he had ever heard of it! The teacher and his teaching assistant became very frustrated, because no amount of differentiation seemed to help. Jason also became frustrated, because he liked Science and the teacher and wanted to do well in it.

When I worked with Jason, it became apparent that he could make little sense of his early years, moving continually between his father and mother's family and each time coming back to a different family configuration. He had been back and forth between primary schools and could not recall where he had been at what age. With so little order and logic in his life, it was not surprising he found the concepts hard to grasp.

I worked with the Science teacher on worksheets which involved only deciding if the answers were true/false - thus establishing only two categories. Then Jason and his TA worked at making a timeline of his own life to try to establish some sense of order. Jason slowly began to be able to put his own life in order and tell a coherent story. Eventually this led to some progress in Science and he was able to sit his SATs exams, even managing to move up a level.

Maths

For some children, Maths can be a strange subject, as it involves thinking about whole things, parts of wholes, adding up, taking away and generally accepting the idea of splitting being okay. For those who have fragmented, complex, confusing family relationships, there can be an unconscious resistance to the idea of breaking up things, adding and taking away for no reason. For others, the idea of adding and subtracting can be alarming as there have been so many examples of loss and complexity in their relationships.

This may be worth bearing in mind with a child who seems unable to apply the basic concepts. It can be helpful to simply say something like: *"I know it can be hard to understand that in maths you can take away and replace things, whereas in life you cannot."*

On the other hand, for other children, Maths can seem safe. Right and wrong is clear. There is a structure and a process which leads to a right or wrong answer. The world seems clear and unambiguous, and this may provide comfort in an otherwise upsettingly uncertain world.

PAUSE FOR THOUGHT

Take a few moments and think about a pupil you find challenging to teach

What are the behaviours which you find troublesome?

Are any of these behaviours similar to those of the pupils described above?

Are you aware of any life circumstances which could be affecting your pupil's ability to learn? Notice if you are being drawn into behaving in a certain way? What can you do when this starts to happen?

Could the issue be with the unconscious feelings stirred up by your subject?

If so, how does this affect your thinking about their behaviour?

Having looked at what can make it hard for 'unteachable' pupils to settle to learn, in the next chapter I will be describing in more detail the ways in which we, the teachers, can be affected by unconscious processes in operation in our classrooms.

In summary

Children who have experienced loss and trauma may not have developed the skills of a good learner

- In particular they may not
  - be willing to take risks
  - have good self-esteem
  - be able to ask for help without fear of humiliation or ridicule
  - be able to manage the frustration of not knowing something
  - be able to wait for attention and trust the adult will remember them

- They may have learned to be hyper-vigilant, to be on constant lookout for potential dangers or changes in the attitudes of the adults around them, making it impossible to focus on the task of learning

- Their early childhood experiences may have affected significant parts of their brains, in particular the connections responsible for empathy, logic and cause/effect

- High levels of stress hormones, notably cortisol, impair the growth and development of the brain

- Their brain patterns and responses will not automatically change with new, positive experiences. The paths will have been laid down from an early age and become embedded in their behaviour

- There are certain patterns of behaviour which we may notice with children who have suffered loss, domestic violence, parental addiction or mental illness. These unconscious learned responses will be played out in school in relationship to teachers
- The actual curriculum can seem scary and challenge these children on an unconscious level, as it may stir up memories of their traumatic early experiences. Their seemingly inexplicable reactions may be linked to these unconscious processes

Chapter 6

Unconscious defence mechanisms

What is going on under the surface in our classrooms?

HOW WE ARE AFFECTED BY THESE CHILDREN

In trying to understand what is happening in our classrooms with these 'unteachable' children, I have found it helpful to apply certain ideas from therapeutic thinking. As I have said previously, there are ideas from the world of therapy which can help us find other explanations for inexplicable behaviour (rather than simply that the pupil is bad or mad or 'doing it deliberately to annoy us'). Such ideas may also offer us more collaborative ways of working with the child, without the need for every teacher to go off and re-train as a therapist. Our aim needs to be to modify the pupil's problematic responses and decrease their anxiety levels. A child or young person often cannot explain why they have chosen to act in a seemingly destructive or challenging way. The preceding chapters have shown that it is rarely possible to address the behaviour only by looking at what is directly observable. We need to learn to observe and think about interactions at the level of the unconscious processes at work.

In this chapter I will focus particularly on the idea of psychological defence mechanisms, which kick into action when we feel under threat or are overly anxious. These ideas are based on the work of Anna Freud, whose training as a teacher and psychoanalyst meant that she was particularly interested in psychoanalytic ideas and education. Unlike some other psychoanalysts, such as Melanie Klein, she believed it was possible to be an analyst and an educator at the same time (Freud, 1973).

PSYCHOLOGICAL DEFENCE MECHANISMS

PROJECTION

When we have unbearable, painful feelings, we may unconsciously externalise them, 'pushing them out' and trying to attribute them to others. We cannot bear to think about them and therefore are 'looking' for another person to 'hold' them, to have them and take them away from us. This is not something which happens only with troubled children and young people. It is something that happens to all of us in our daily life when we try to manage very difficult and painful feelings. It is a process which begins with infants when they feel overwhelmed by unknown feelings and project them out so that someone else, usually the mother, will be able to help them make sense of their feelings and provide reassurance.

The Jelly Bean Tree

I used to run an on-site unit for pupils who were being given a 'last chance' and were at risk of permanent exclusion from school. Sometimes at the end of the week, I would feel completely depressed and useless as a teacher. I realised that I had spent my week with children and young people who felt depressed, hopeless and useless. It seemed as if they had projected their feelings into me and were giving me a very powerful experience of what it was like to be them.

I had asked the young people to do a presentation about the work we did with them. At the end of a presentation where they showed a task called the 'Jelly Bean Tree', David said "This is a tree which shows how we feel. At the beginning of working with Miss Delaney, we were at the bottom and she was at the top, now we are at the top and I think at times she feels she is at the bottom!" It was a great reminder of what happens in the projection of feelings, and shows that young people can recognise it too!

Implications for the teacher

How you are feeling when you're with a child may give you an indication of what they are feeling. The task is to recognise which feelings are your own and which are projected. Feelings need to be contained (that is, thought about by a caring, well-intentioned adult to make them feel manageable, *see* p.124) named, and perhaps at an appropriate time, 'reflected back' in a 'digested', acceptable form. 'Reflecting back' means the process of trying to recognise the way a pupil is feeling, often by noticing how you are left feeling in your interactions with them, and putting a name to it in your conversation with the pupil. By 'digesting' the feelings, I am suggesting that we need to hold onto our ability to think about them, even if they are very negative and overwhelming. We then need to put the feelings into words, thus making them less terrifying.

Obviously, being the 'recipient' of strongly negative feelings is not easy. It can be tempting, and indeed seem normal, to want to retaliate or attack with our own strong feelings. If we act in the moment, without taking time to think and reflect, we may find ourselves getting angry, upset or even aggressive with pupils who are pouring their feelings out onto us.

But if we project the feelings back to the pupil in the same way and with the same intensity, they may cause terror and what Bion calls 'nameless dread' (Bion, 1962). The baby who cries uncontrollably and is then shouted at, is having his or her painful feelings intensified and not held or understood. Similarly, the pupil who is raging at the teacher and who eventually provokes an angry reaction is having his feelings magnified and returned, thus learning that the adult is also unable to bear such strong feelings.

Caroline's struggle to stay calm

Stephen is a year 9 pupil who is presently living in a refuge for families affected by domestic violence. He gets very angry in many of his classes and shouts at teachers, saying that no-one likes him and he hates their lessons.

Caroline, the Deputy Head often has to deal with Stephen on discipline issues, and knows that the best strategy is to remain calm and not engage in arguments with him, as this only adds fuel to his fire. However, she says: "I nearly always end up shouting angrily at Stephen, no matter how hard I try to remain calm. I realise that I am raising my voice and telling him that he won't last much longer in this school if he continues misbehaving. I cringe when I hear myself saying it and it only makes him angrier than ever. And yet, it always seems to happen."

The overwhelming feeling does not have to be anger. It can happen that we find ourselves telling a demotivated student that we "*can't be bothered, if he can't be bothered*". Again, we are getting caught in a situation where we are sending the feeling of demotivation back to the student, and probably intensifying it.

Similarly, we can do this with our own feelings. We may attribute feelings to young people which, in fact, 'belong' to us.

A teacher who had just come back to school after a few days' bereavement leave was telling her colleagues in the staffroom that all her classes seemed lethargic and demotivated, as if they could not be bothered to do anything. Her colleagues thought that this might be a reflection of her current mood: she was, after all, quite depressed after her recent bereavement. They had not noticed any change in the general mood of the pupils.

Learning a little about projection helped me to understand what was going on and to discuss this with pupils and staff such as those described above. As a classroom teacher, it can be a relief to realise that not everything you feel may be 'coming from' you. Being able to think about your experience, and what might be happening with your pupils, before responding or designing an intervention, can give you a wider range of options.

> *"I was really happy to learn about the concept of projection. It made me feel better about myself and classes I find difficult. I always thought it was my fault and I was just not good enough as a teacher. It's a relief to realise it is not all my fault and that some of these things just happen for other reasons."* Recently qualified primary teacher in a workshop, on learning about the idea of projection

What can the teacher do?

- ✔ Be aware of any overwhelming or inexplicable feelings which you might be experiencing when with certain classes or pupils. Take a moment to consider where the feeling has come from.
- ✔ If you think it is giving you some information about the pupil, acknowledge this and, if appropriate, name it for the young person. For example, you might say to the class, "*It feels as if we are getting a bit stuck now and I'm beginning to feel a bit fed up. Perhaps some of you are feeling like that and we need to try something different.*"
- ✔ You may need to take a moment and deliberately change your own and perhaps the class's emotional and physical state. Do an activity which changes the energy in the room. For example, a physical stretching exercise or a quick team quiz to review main learning points.
- ✔ If possible, take some time and discuss the feeling with a colleague. It might be cathartic to realise other people are having the same experience and you might be able to share strategies for dealing with it.

TRANSFERENCE

The unconscious phenomenon known as transference may be at work, when, for example, feelings and attitudes from a relationship with a child's main carers from the past are 'transferred' and are played out, or re-experienced, in a later relationship with a teacher.

Some examples of this are -

- the child who seems to go out of their way to cross the path of a teacher with whom they continually have conflict
- the child who seems to take an instant dislike to a new teacher, despite their best efforts to engage them

Transference can be triggered by all kinds of things, for example, a look, a tone of voice, a way of dressing, a role, even a way of walking. It occurs because we are trying to understand someone (usually someone we do not know very well) by making an assumption that they are similar to someone else whom we know. It is a fundamental process which happens to all of us in our attempts to make sense of our relationships with other people.

Be aware that this can work the other way round as well. A teacher can find themselves reacting badly to a particular pupil with no apparent reason; the child or young person may be triggering a reminder of the teacher's relationship with, for example, their own child or sibling.

Mr Buckley and Patrick

Mr Buckley, the Head of Year and a certain pupil, Patrick, were constantly in conflict. Despite numerous attempts to mediate and find a solution, they would inevitably end up in a dispute sometime during the school day. These conflicts could be about small things, such as whether a note from home had been passed on or not, and about things which other students were allowed to do, for example, go home early for exam study.

The Head of Year's assistant commented to me that she thought it was because Mr Buckley was having trouble at home with his own teenage son, and felt very powerless about helping him. It seemed on some level he could only take back control in his interactions with Patrick. The Head of Year had admitted to feeling powerless in getting his own son to listen to him or to take his advice. In fact he was worried that he might be self-harming. There seemed to be something in Patrick's attitude which sparked off a connection for him.

With this in mind, I was able to have a discussion with Mr Buckley about how transference can affect us. Although not completely convinced, he did say it gave him pause for thought. Without realising it, he appeared to have been replaying the relationship in school, where he had the power to 'win' by sending the young person home - even though there were only six weeks to go to the exams and he had told staff that he wanted them to do their best to keep students in school.

Implications for the teacher

A pupil's seeming inexplicable reaction to a member of staff may be triggered by who they remind the child of. Our own reaction to a child may relate to our own previous experience of a different relationship. Gerda Hanko, in her teacher support groups (Hanko 1999) encourages teachers to think *"It's not meant for me"*, rather than the usual - *"Don't take it personally"*, which can be very hard when you're in the firing line! I've found this to be an extremely helpful way of re-framing what is happening.

As a teacher you can work with this transference, and try to give the child an experience of a different way of relating. If we begin to notice the pattern of interaction, we may be able to stop ourselves being 'pulled in' and do something different to break the pattern, with the hope of averting the predictable negative outcome.

George and the Head of Maths

George is thirteen years old. He had spent much of his primary schooling outside the Headteacher's office as he was continually disruptive in class. From the beginning of secondary school staff found him increasingly difficult to deal with.

Work with George in the LSU allowed him to calm down and attend most lessons. However, despite everyone's best efforts, he still had on-going conflict with the Head of Maths. The Head of Maths had come to me and said that he was doing his best to use the strategies suggested to him, but that George continually tried to provoke him into sending him out of class. A member of the support staff confirmed this was happening.

I thought about the kind of teacher this man was and what might be happening in terms of transference. He was a strict teacher, with very clear boundaries and beliefs. I wondered if this was the type of father-figure George had experienced or wanted to experience.

*I spoke about this to George and the teacher. They were both unimpressed by the idea. In fact, after both conversations, I wondered if there had been any point in re-framing it like this! The teacher had said "Not sure if I believe in all that psycho-babble, Marie." George said "No way, who'd want that *** for a father!" !!*

However, despite my doubts, things seemed to improve between them. I think that this type of 'wondering aloud', about what might be going on between them, did cause a shift in their relationship.

(This technique is discussed in more detail in Chapter 10, on developing teaching skills)

DISPLACEMENT

This happens when an emotion we are feeling about a particular relationship or person in our life cannot be safely expressed toward that person, but is displaced onto another person or into another situation. Take a moment to think about a time when something has happened at work which has made you very angry and how you reacted that night at home to a relatively minor comment from your family!

A child who has witnessed domestic violence will often have very mixed emotions about their parents. They might be sorry for the victim, usually the mother, but also very angry at her for allowing the violence to take place. Equally, they will feel angry at their own helplessness and disrespect. They will also love their mother and not want to have these feelings. These complex feelings are often displaced onto a strong attachment figure, most likely a teacher in class. It is safer to rant and rave and tell a teacher you hate them and that they're stupid, than it is to verbalise these feelings at home. Of course, this nearly always happens on the day when you, the teacher, are feeling particularly useless and stupid!

Some examples of this are

→ the child who has witnessed or is witnessing domestic violence, who reacts angrily to teachers

→ the child who is anxious about leaving their depressed parent or carer at home alone, who displaces the anxiety into a separation anxiety about going to school. He or she may become school-phobic, and cite lots of seemingly untrue examples of how bad school has been

→ the bully who uses power over children at school because he or she is powerless at home, and has displaced his or her power-seeking behaviour to school

Unlike therapy with adults, the parent is also present in the child's environment and feelings for them mingle with feelings for you. Anna Freud talks about the therapist sharing the child's 'hostile and loving impulses' with the parents (Freud, 1973). Sometimes it might seem as if the teacher and adults in the school are the receptacle for all sorts of hostile feelings and actions.

Implications for the teacher

If you feel you are on the receiving end of an inexplicable, overwhelming emotion, take some time to think about it in terms of displacement. Who might the young person be angry with or where might it come from originally? If appropriate, you might ask, *"What exactly are you angry about?"* Sometimes it is appropriate to comment in general, *"Sometimes people get very angry at someone when they are angry about a lot of other things and situations"*. This is easier to hear than a specific message that anger may be being displaced from the pupil's relationship with another key person in their life. Children who act in all-powerful ways at school may in fact be powerless at home.

Billy's pent-up feelings

Billy was a fifteen year old boy, recently transferred from another school in the area. He had already had several incidents with staff and pupils in which he had got uncontrollably angry, swearing, threatening to kill people and shouting abuse. He repeatedly stated that he did not want to stay at this school and would soon be going back to his old school. We were aware that this was not going to happen. He was not liked by his peers who found him 'strange'. Staff also found him unlikeable and thought that he just "didn't care".

It was very difficult to work with Billy as he would continually tell the staff that he did not need any help. It felt important to try to withstand this assault without jumping into discussions where we tried to reassure Billy that we could help him. Initially he often spent time with myself, the Head of Year or another member of SLT, because no-one else felt they could deal with him in class. We focused on simple, non-emotive activities in those times. What he was saying did not seem to reflect his underlying anxieties. He often tried to provoke a persecutory or blaming attitude from us, and it seemed important to show him a different experience, one of a non-judgmental observer, who witnessed his actions and words and sometimes tried to put a name to the feelings.

He was keen to have his mum come into the school. It proved difficult to meet her, as she often cancelled appointments. When she did eventually come in, he went home and refused to attend the meeting. Understandably, this exasperated the staff dealing with him. However, we had to think about what this meant. Who was he angry with? Subsequently, it became apparent that it was displaced anger towards his mother, which he wanted to show us by not attending the meeting with her.

In a later meeting Billy's mother told me that previously she had been in an abusive relationship, and that Billy had seen a lot of domestic violence. This gave me a way of looking at Billy's behaviour. I felt he was unconsciously re-enacting the violence of his past, at times empathising with the aggressor. He would also never admit to any misdemeanour, even when witnessed by several people. When I felt we had developed a relationship, I commented to him that often the children of domestic violence tell lies because they have to try to avoid being hit themselves. Although he rubbished this comment at the time, he began to talk more about his past.

We read some children's stories, in particular 'A Pea Called Mildred' by Margot Sunderland (Sunderland,1999), a story about a pea that wanted to be different. I talked about how this pea wanted to be different in a positive way, and how it was okay to stand out from the crowd. Billy again rubbished this story but often mentioned it to me in later discussions. I felt he could cope with the interpretation of the characters in the story, which reflected his fears and anxieties about being different.

Eventually Billy wrote an autobiographical account of his life. In this he detailed very specifically many incidents of violence and domestic abuse, and how he had felt at the time. We were able to talk about his feelings of helplessness and anger towards his mother for allowing it to happen, and towards himself for not being able to protect her. He wanted to share this story with key staff who had to deal with him when he was in trouble.

What can the teacher do?

It was very important for Billy that staff continued to try to understand his behaviour and not 'buy into' his patterns. He drew aggressive responses onto himself because that is what he knew and was comfortable with. Staff who did not see him as 'strange', and tried to give a name to some of what he might be feeling, helped Billy unravel his story. The role of class teachers here was to remain positive in their dealings with Billy, and to understand that a lot of his anger was not directed towards them.

When Billy shared his story with key members of staff, it was important that they found a way to react which acknowledged the difficult feelings and situations in the story, but did not suggest that they were overwhelmed and unable to cope with the information. Even if we feel very shocked and upset by a story such as Billy's, we can show him that such feelings can be managed and withstood. This will be the beginning of Billy realising he also can think about the meaning of his story, and reflect on his own feelings about it.

This is not easy. Sometimes our natural reaction is to avoid thinking about these feelings and to concentrate, for example, on marking the punctuation and paragraphing in a traumatic autobiography, making no reference to the emotions in the content.

Why is this? I do not think it is because teachers are unfeeling human beings. In fact, it is probably the opposite. It can be hard to cope with thinking about these pupils' stories, usually because it is overwhelming and painful to think of the feelings evoked.

✔ Simply paying attention to the overwhelming feeling and not rejecting it, and making simple comments on the feeling-tone, can be of vital importance to the young person's emotional development.

I found out later that Billy had at last admitted to something he had done at school, something he had been adamant had not been him, even though a whole class had witnessed what had occurred. He apologised to the teacher and to the pupil. It seemed that telling his story and having it heard may have unlocked some capacity in him to think more rationally and logically. It was possible to maintain Billy in mainstream. Although it was always a bumpy ride, staff felt they had some understanding of where his anger was coming from.

COUNTER-TRANSFERENCE

We can get caught up in the pattern the child is creating around them. We can see in the example of Billy that we can be drawn into re-enacting a relationship from the child's past. Unfortunately, we can often find ourselves, for example, becoming angry and aggressive to children who have experienced domestic violence, almost as if we are 'playing the part' of the abuser. It is vital that we become aware of these processes, known in therapy terms as one aspect of counter-transference, and break the pattern. We need to ensure we do not get pulled into this kind of behaviour, and give children such as Billy a new experience.

Implications for the teacher

The concept of transference and counter-transference may help us to realise that there are times when problems arise in our interactions with pupils which are not predictable or caused by our actions. Recognising this might stop us agonizing about what we did wrong in situations where a pupil's, or indeed adult's, reaction seems to have been completely out of proportion to the trigger event or request (for example, we ask a student to move seats and she storms out of the room, shouting that we always pick on her).

What can the teacher do?

As a teacher, it is not possible to completely avoid examples of transference and counter-transference. Sometimes we get caught up in them without realising.

- ✔ However, it is important to try to notice it when it is happening so that we can make efforts to break the pattern that is developing.
- ✔ Take a step back when you find this happening in class, give yourself time to acknowledge your feeling and pay attention to it.
- ✔ We can also become more aware of our own potential triggers and learn to manage them.
- ✔ We need to remember that the pupil is not the same as the person from our past, and try to focus on what is different in our reaction to them, so that we can develop a different way of relating.

SPLITTING

Children with emotional and behavioural difficulties tend to polarize people and opinions. This can also be seen as the defence mechanism of splitting, a way of dealing with anxiety. The child unconsciously protects itself from difficult feelings by starting to view people as either all bad or all good, rather than a mixture of the two.

Being able to recognise that people are made up of different parts and that that is okay, is an important part of a child's development. Children can learn to realise that their parent or caregiver can love them *and* still be cross sometimes. The child learns that the teacher can sometimes be annoyed or shout, but this is not a catastrophe and does not mean they hate the children. Children and young people with a background of trauma, loss, neglect and abuse find it hard to believe they or anyone else can be made up of different parts. They talk about being 'good' or 'bad'. If something goes wrong, they see it as a disaster, and they often go on to behave appallingly as they cannot believe that a setback can be viewed favourably. They cannot believe that the teacher will not continue to regard them positively if they have done something wrong once again.

When a pupil who is feeling highly anxious starts to behave in a very challenging way, the adults working with the child can find themselves blaming each other, or feeling (or even saying) that they are the only person helping this child. They are experiencing the splitting process, rather than being able to focus on working together to find ways to help the pupil.

We should remember that splitting is not a phenomenon limited to children. It happens in all kinds of groups and organisations when people feel frightened, excessively anxious or under attack. You will see examples of it in friendship groups, families, organisations and, of course, at an international level when countries go to war.

When splitting happens in schools, it can impede our ability to work collaboratively. This has often happened to me when I have been working with a pupil who is at risk of exclusion. I have found myself thinking very negatively about certain staff members, thinking there is no point in discussing the students with them, as *"They have no empathy, they just believe in punishment"*. I have come to recognise that this is an example of splitting, caused by the overwhelming feelings of frustration around children and young people with traumatic early experiences.

We have probably all sat in meetings where we have complained that some other agency or person has not done all they could to help a particular child. This is often because the feelings around the child have split us, preventing us from integrating and working together effectively.

Implications for the teacher

Being conscious of this phenomenon is important when dealing with other members of staff or organisations working with these children and young people. If you can recognise splitting when it is happening, you can work to minimise it by consciously working together to find solutions, rather than apportioning blame.

What can the teacher do?

✔ It may be useful at the start of staff meetings and inter-agency meetings to state how difficult it is to think about these children. If someone can name the feelings evoked by the pupil's situation, it can alleviate the need for defence by splitting. For example, you could say:

"It is very difficult to think about these pupils, perhaps we all feel a bit helpless and as if we are failing"

✔ When discussing these pupils, work on noticing what is working, and try not to fall into blaming others for a lack of solutions. Be careful that you are not blaming people who are not present for the situation.

✔ If you find yourself in conflict with another member of staff about the best way to deal with a pupil, ask yourself if this is an example of splitting and find a way to discuss shared strategies.

✔ Set up support groups around the child or young person, so everyone involved can focus on helping each other.

OMNIPOTENCE

In school, children who feel powerless or have little control over their lives can act as if they need to control and know everything. They find it hard to be taught because they cannot accept the state of *not knowing*: it reminds them of their vulnerability. They do not want the teacher to have the power of knowing more than them, which can feel like power *over* them. If they do not allow the teacher to teach them, they will not have to experience this vulnerability. Staff can get very frustrated at not being able to 'help' or 'teach' them. Paradoxically, omnipotence as a defence often stems from feeling totally anxious, fearful, unsafe and not in control of your own life.

Sally's sabotage (Part 2)

Sally (the eleven year old mentioned on p.34) was considered at risk of exclusion, and staff were at a loss with how to deal with her. She refused to attend most lessons, often standing in the corridor outside class and being verbally abusive to anyone who tried to talk to her. When she did attend a class, she was unable to pay attention to the teacher for long, being continually involved in other people's work and conversation.

She continually accused staff of persecuting her and blaming her unfairly. Staff were often drawn into asserting control in a punitive way, thus making her internal fantasies real. She often told me that I was rubbish at my job and should stop wasting my time. Of course, this fed into a thought I had often had myself! She was very controlling, and wanted to dictate to everyone in the group. Although appearing to be of at least average ability, she seemed unable to learn to read.

The breakthrough with Sally came when she became interested in a role-play we were preparing for an assembly. It involved pupils taking the part of a teacher and an unruly class. When she took on the role of the teacher she became a very controlling, authoritarian figure, overly punitive and persecutory. When she took on the role of a pupil she became very immature and babyish, giggling, crawling around, sucking her thumb and becoming at times practically hysterical.

It was tempting to be drawn into the punitive role and stop Sally taking part, but by taking some time to reflect on what her behaviour might be showing, it became apparent that this type of activity was allowing her to act out her inner world. After the assembly, she often wanted to do role-plays and act out situations which involved her in the role of a very powerful figure. It seemed that her inner world was full of anxieties and feelings of envy and persecution. She could not allow staff to teach her. She could not 'bear to be little'. (Emmanuel, in Ward 1995, p.54) .

Sally often wanted to play games with other pupils but would inevitably spoil them by cheating. We began to incorporate card games and competitive games into the curriculum, so that she could fulfill her aggressive desires in a safe way, and we could comment on the difficulty of allowing other people to win or know more. It was important not to comment directly on what was happening, but to use more general language such as "It can feel very difficult to lose or to let other people have a go. Some people feel this is like letting them take over everything."

Eventually Sally was able to take part in an alternative curriculum which included successful work experience placements. Her 'blow-ups' became less frequent and more manageable.

Implications for the teacher

If the defence of omnipotence is in operation, it may feel as if you are engaging in a battle of wills with a pupil over who is in control of the class. You may find yourself refusing even reasonable requests, and thinking, "*I'm the teacher, not him*". The pupil will need boundaries from you, and space to feel they have some control of their situation. If we are not careful, we can find ourselves fighting unnecessary battles.

Simon's independent learning

Simon was a high-achieving pupil in year 11, but was very difficult to manage in class as he seemed to want to dictate the content and pace of the lesson. The Head of Science was heard complaining in the staffroom because Simon has asked him for the Science revision books and he did not hand these out until the end of the winter term. When he had time to think about it, he realised that this was a ridiculous conflict, as usually he was delighted if any student wanted to get ahead with their revision!

What can the teacher do?

✔ It is important that all staff try to see beyond the seemingly impossible behaviour of children such as Sally, above, and to understand why a child might have a NEED to control everything. It was important not to reject Sally in the way that she was rejecting us.

✔ You may be thinking that some of the work described above is not possible in class, but it is possible, as a mainstream teacher, to try to understand what the behaviour is showing about internal anxieties and fantasies which are getting in the way of learning.

✔ It is also, I feel, possible to incorporate activities into a lesson which allow for safe expression of these feelings.

✔ Practising the art of commenting generally on what the underlying need might be, is a very useful technique for the classroom teacher (*see* pp.158-9 *for more on commenting*).

✔ Wherever possible, hand over some control on negotiable things, for example, the order of some tasks. Build in choices where the pupil can choose between two ways of completing the same topic.

SPOILING

Some children seem determined to spoil things for themselves and others. This can be very frustrating to observe in class, as the child will often act as if the lesson is worthless and the work produced is rubbish. As with omnipotence (*see above*), this can be a defence against the frustration of not knowing something and feeling envious of those who do - in particular, the teacher. Because the child might be envious of the teacher's knowledge, on some unconscious level they will not want the teacher to be allowed to show this knowledge, to teach them, so they are unconsciously driven to 'spoil' the teacher's abilities or sense of competence. Spoiling can also happen when the child is anxious about taking the risk of learning, of getting it wrong or of gaining a different perspective on themselves as a learner. It may be difficult for some children and young people to take the risk of learning, as they might have tried to cross this bridge before and failed.

Moving Michael

Michael, aged ten, seemed capable but spent much of his time acting out. Other children described him as a 'nutter' and teachers were wary of dealing with him as they felt he 'might do anything', and took too many risks. I noticed that Michael's pattern was to behave so outrageously and often dangerously that he was sent out of class or allowed to sit at the back and not work. I wondered what was so dangerous about learning.

In my first meeting with Michael, I decided to name what I thought was going on. I said that I had noticed that he often behaved in such a mad way that teachers left him alone. I said that in my work with him, I was going to assume that he was not a 'nutter' and that he could behave normally. I would assume that about him whatever he did.

Michael was surprised. He then spent several weeks challenging me to break this assumption, for example, entering rooms on all fours, sitting under tables instead of at them on a chair, swinging on doors singing "I shall not be moved" when a teacher asked that he be removed from a lesson, climbing onto window sills and doing forward rolls onto the chair cushions.

At times it was very difficult not to retaliate and tell him not to be so stupid and to stop doing it. I tried to name what I thought he was doing and interrupt or change his pattern. For example, one day I got under the table when he was trying to be sensible and asked him how he felt when I did this. I asked him how many times he thought he would have to do the forward rolls off the window sill before he could settle to work. He was so surprised that he stopped. He got fed up with it all before I did.

Implications for the teacher

It can be very depressing and demotivating to teach pupils when spoiling is in evidence. You can feel like you are not having any success with the pupil, are seemingly unable to teach them or see any improvement in their learning. Some of these pupils can actually seem quite compliant in the lesson but never actually make any progress. It is tempting to give up or accept a lower standard of work from pupils who do this.

What can the teacher do?

You may need to set up ways for these pupils to attempt the work and have the opportunity to revise and re-draft it. Laminated wipe-clean boards are useful, as the pupil does not have to commit his answers permanently to the paper and can feel that the risk of getting it wrong is minimised. Wondering aloud is also a useful technique here. You might say :

"It feels unbearable to take the risk of getting it wrong and trusting me to teach you".

"I'm wondering if you are feeling fed up now because you were not picked to answer any questions, even though you remembered to put your hand up."

I am not suggesting that, in a classroom on an everyday basis, you can do the kind of extreme pattern-matching I described in the example of working with Michael. However, you can use the principle of trying to recognise the pattern being set up, not being drawn into it and doing something to interrupt the pattern. It does not really matter what you do, just that you do something different.

In summary

In our teaching of 'unteachable' children and young people, we need to be aware of underlying unconscious defence mechanisms evoked in us and them. An understanding of these may lead us to think differently about what is happening. Part of our role is to help the child observe and make sense of his responses.

- Be aware of feelings which may be being projected onto you. They may give you an indication of how the child or young person is feeling
- Schools and teachers can provide emotional holding
- Teachers can provide recognition and affirmation of feelings
- If a child is triggering a repeated response from you, think about the idea of transference and counter-transference. Could it be a reminder of a previous relationship pattern of yours or theirs?

(continues ...)

- Are you 'buying into' the pattern? Break the pattern. Do anything as long as it is not what is expected or what your initial feelings are being drawn towards doing

- Find ways to comment indirectly - *"I'm wondering if..."* or *"some people find it unbearable to..."*

- Be aware that splitting and polarisation of views can happen around a child. The intensity of emotions can lead adults to take up extreme views. Avoid the 'blame' approach and work to keep a joined-up thinking approach with other staff and agencies

- Children need to learn a tolerance of loss and limitations - and maybe we do too

- Children who want to control everything may be exhibiting a defence against the anxiety of being powerless in other areas of their life. They may feel fearful and unsafe, rather than omnipotent as they appear. See this as displaying a need rather an attempt to 'have everything their own way'

- Children who are deliberately hurtful or spoil things for others may be showing an envy of others' ability to learn or even accept help

- Commenting indirectly or wondering aloud can help ease an anxiety by putting a name to it. It is not necessary to be able to interpret it at this stage

- Find ways to show the child they are being held in mind and thought about. We learn to think by being thought about.

Chapter 7

Attachment theory
The implications for learning

I have found it useful to think about some of the children I have worked with from the perspective of what is known as 'Attachment theory', drawn from the work of John Bowlby (1969, 1972, 1988) and Mary Ainsworth (1969). Whilst not providing 'the answer' to all of these 'unteachable' children's problems, I do believe this body of research can give us a useful way of looking at what is happening with them. From this perspective, we will be in a better position to develop additional and more effective strategies for working with them in our schools. For the purpose of this book, I will first introduce the broad concepts of Attachment theory which I have found most helpful as a classroom teacher, linking patterns of attachment to Geddes' 'Learning Triangle'. For a more detailed description of the links between Attachment theory and learning, see Geddes (2006)

To conclude this chapter, I will also discuss containment, the way in which we, as teachers, can show pupils that overwhelming, often painful feelings, can be acknowledged, given a name and thus may become less frightening. By showing the pupil that we can think about these types of feelings, we can begin to help him or her to manage them appropriately.

CORE CONCEPTS OF ATTACHMENT THEORY

A child's expectation of being cared for, thought about and helped in a loving way develops as a result of their early experience, and will subsequently affect their ability to learn. A key concept of Attachment theory is that infants are pre-programmed to develop attachment behaviour to their primary caregiver - usually the mother. Attachment behaviour describes the way in which infant and mother negotiate a way of responding to each other in the early months of a child's life. The aim of this attachment behaviour is proximity or contact with the attachment figure, with the associated feelings of safety and security.

If the baby can obtain this proximity and contact, he or she can use this relationship as a 'secure base' from which to develop (*see below*). The baby seeks attachment and returns to the secure base, when he or she feels alarm, upset or anxious. The young child learns about his own feelings by the response they elicit. If he cries when he is hungry and is fed, he learns to expect this response. The mother also uses words to try to name what might be going on. When the mother is able to respond, pay attention to these needs, and give a name to her baby's feelings, the feelings can be 'contained' and do not become overwhelming for the child. Containment implies that the mother has recognised, understood, thought about and if appropriate, 'reflected back' her baby's feelings in a manageable way. For example, when a baby cries, the mother may pick him up, suggesting what might be happening - *"I know, you are frightened, that was a very loud noise, wasn't it? You thought I had gone away, but Mummy's here"*.

When the mother's response is fairly consistent, the child learns to trust that this is an adult behaviour he or she can expect. Children with this experience develop internal worlds where there is a representation of an attachment figure, a secure adult, who will not reject or humiliate them when they need understanding.

Separation and learning

The child can thus develop the confidence to 'separate' from the caregiver and develop a sense of self, secure in the knowledge that they are still being thought about in their absence. They come to learn that a separation can be tolerated without the world falling apart, as they have a secure memory of this containment and responsive interaction. This separation of mother and child needs to take place because learning can only occur in the separate space between the child and the adult. The child can develop the sense of being curious and able to explore new things, capacities central to being able to learn.

The four patterns of attachment

Bowlby's work (1969, 1972, 1988) was developed further by Mary Ainsworth, (1969) who found four patterns of attachment behaviour could be observed in children:

- securely attached
- insecure/ambivalent-resistant
- insecure/avoidant
- insecure/disorganised

Understanding how patterns of attachment affect children's ability to learn will enable us to think in a different way about their needs, how we can plan to meet these needs and thus develop teaching strategies based on our observation of these attachment patterns. The Learning Triangle (Geddes 2006) provides a useful framework for us to integrate Attachment theory with classroom learning and the relationships which take place between teacher, pupil and task.

THE LEARNING TRIANGLE

In any learning experience, there is a triangle between teacher, pupil and task (*see below*). In order to learn, the pupil needs to feel secure and trust the relationship with the teacher. However, he or she also needs to be able to separate from the teacher and work on the task, secure in the knowledge that the teacher is available to provide help and support when required. Children who have not experienced this type of relationship with an adult in their early life can find it very difficult to make space inside themselves for the task of learning.

For example, some children or young people may be over-anxious about maintaining and checking out the relationship with the teacher, continually seeking her reassurance and attention, and unable to focus on any learning task which might distract them from this focus. Such behaviour could be categorised as one of the patterns of insecure attachment, ambivalent-resistant (*see* p.106). Other pupils may be unable to trust the relationship with their teacher: they have learned that they might be rejected in their attempts to seek attachment. These children will only be able to focus on the task, refusing to interact and accept help or teaching when needed. This might represent an insecure/avoidant pattern of attachment (*see* p.111). I will look at each of the four patterns of attachment in more detail, in relation to how they affect classroom learning.

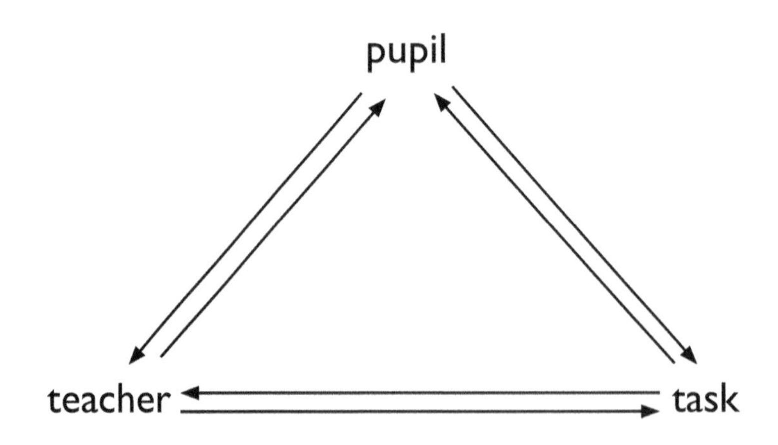

(Geddes 2006, p.4)

SECURE ATTACHMENT

Securely attached children develop basic trust and confidence that others will be helpful when asked. They generally cope better in schools since, within the context of their early relationships, they have learned the skills highlighted earlier (*see* p.61) as essential to being a good learner. They can usually play independently, take risks, ask for help, wait for attention and relate positively to peers and teachers. They are safe in their trust of the relationship with the adult and can therefore focus on the task. Generally, their Learning Triangle is in balance. At an early stage in their lives, they have had an experience of being thought about, and their overwhelming feelings have been managed by an adult care-giver.

Over time, securely attached babies and young children do better in terms of:

Self-esteem
Independence and autonomy
Resilience in the face of adversity
Ability to manage impulses and feelings
Long-term friendships
Social coping skills
Relationships with parents, caregivers and other authority figures
Trust, intimacy and affection
Empathy, compassion and conscience
Positive and hopeful belief systems about self, family and society
Behavioural performance and academic success

(Levy, 1998, cited in Bomber 2007)

INSECURE ATTACHMENT

Children who have not had an experience of a secure attachment in their early years may struggle at school. For whatever reason, they have not experienced a sense of being thought about, having an adult 'attuned' to their needs and able to contain their emotions, or having their needs met adequately. They might have been left to cry or been shouted at when they were in distress. Their needs may sometimes have been attended to, and sometimes not. In general, their attempts to seek attachment have been rejected. Ainsworth (1969) identified three main patterns of insecure attachment.

INSECURE AND AMBIVALENT/RESISTANT PATTERN

These children cannot predict their mother's response and so are reluctant to leave her side. An infant who has been rebuffed, not picked up or put down when seeking consolation, will often increase his or her attempts to get a response. The child might become clingy, constantly seeking reassurance that they are cared for. This kind of insecure attachment may arise when the caregiver has suffered from addiction or been subjected to domestic violence. For whatever reasons, there were times when the caregiver was emotionally and physically available and other times when they were not. The child's attempts to connect with an adult are fuelled by anxiety and a need to check out the relationship. In school, they may sometimes continue to seem more helpless than they really are, because they want to keep the connection with a key adult.

How do we see this in class?

Jane (Part 2)

Jane, whom we met on p.68, is in year 8. We saw that she is desperate for Mr Marshall's attention throughout the lesson, continually craving individual interaction with him. She volunteers loudly for all kinds of helping tasks and often gets into disputes in the lesson when another pupil wants to help as well. Even though most of the teachers can understand that Jane is insecure and needs their attention, they find her behaviour irritating and exhausting. Jane always wants to stay behind and help and keeps turning up at the staffroom door at break-times to see if there are any jobs she can do for any of the teachers. She seems very sensitive to what she perceives as rejection and has often burst into tears when it as been gently suggested that she go out with her friends at break. Teachers often find themselves spending a lot of time with Jane and then somehow feeling manipulated into giving up their free time.

What could be happening with Jane?

Jane appears to be exhibiting an insecure/ambivalent-resistant attachment pattern. She cannot focus on the task because she is too worried about maintaining the relationship with teachers. Jane's mother was suffering from drug and alcohol addiction when Jane was born. She made several attempts to come off drugs and at times was able to parent Jane in a safe way. When drinking, however, her moods could become violent or tearful and she was unable to cope with Jane's infant demands. Jane has learned that you cannot trust the mood of adults and that you need to be hyper-vigilant in monitoring the relationship you have with them. She cannot believe that when an adult leaves you, they can still think about you and 'hold you in mind'. She has not had any experience with this. She therefore needs to stay close to the teachers, perceives other young people as competing for the scarce resource of the teacher's attention and cannot take her attention away from the relationship for long enough to do the task.

In school, as we can see with Jane, these children and young people are often -

→ very anxious
→ overly dependent on the teacher
→ unable to take independent action
→ in need of constant reassurance
→ unable to focus on the task in case they lose the attention of the teacher
→ able to use spoken language very skilfully in order to maintain the teacher's attention
→ labelled manipulative
→ those children, who, even when old enough to go out at playtime, refuse to go because they want to stay close to the teacher at all times

Insecure and ambivalent/resistant pattern and the Learning Triangle

In the Learning Triangle, these pupils' focus is on the adult-child relationship, and not the child-task part of the triangle. They are so busy worrying about the relationship that they cannot focus on the task. For them the task is dangerous, as it involves separation and leaving the adult. As they have often had little experience of being thought about, they cannot believe that an adult can think about them and remember them when they are not in close proximity or in the room with them.

This type of child or young person can be very wearing on the teacher's patience and emotional energy, as they are continually working to get the teacher's attention. It does not seem to matter how much positive attention they get, it never seems enough for them. Indeed, they may seem blaming and resentful, holding grudges and saying that the teacher is not fair to them, even when they have had an inordinate amount of extra attention.

Jane's teacher, Mr Marshall, says:

"I know that Jane likes to sit near me and have jobs to do but nothing ever seems enough. Whatever I do, she craves more attention. She can be quite stubborn and want to get her own way. For example, last lesson, when I had given the instructions, I took care to go over and check that Jane knew what to do. She wasn't doing the task, just kept asking me about a job at breaktime. Then I was called over to another student and she kept calling over to me. Eventually I snapped and said "Jane, just wait your turn", and she sulked for the rest of the lesson, getting no work done. Then at lunchtime she came to the staffroom and said she needed to speak to me. I felt so guilty about snapping at her that I came out to talk to her and didn't get my lunch."

What does this behaviour pattern tell us about Jane's needs?

Pupils such as Jane need to develop the required separation from the adult in order to learn and concentrate on the task. They also need some amount of reassurance that this is safe to do and that the adult will still be available as a secure base if help is needed. They have little sense of self as a separate being, and as such would need to have this kind of experience. They need the teacher to show them that they are being held in mind when they are absent, but to learn that it is okay to separate long enough to do the task - and that, if they do this, the relationship will not change.

Teaching strategies

Teaching strategies, therefore, should be designed to meet the needs demonstrated by this attachment-seeking behaviour.

The temptation with these children is to give them what they appear to demand. Often a Teaching Assistant is appointed to sit with them, to ensure they get on with their work. If we are not careful, the Teaching Assistant can be drawn into doing a lot of the work for them. She may resort to constantly nagging the pupil to get on with the task, staying by their side to make sure they keep on track. In the long-term, this is not helping the child or young person develop the required separation for learning to take place. These children may seem as if they cannot learn. It is important not to collude with their behaviour, but to try to understand the anxiety that drives it and find effective ways of acknowledging it and allowing them to settle to learn.

Strategies which might help are therefore those which reassure the child that he or she can be held in mind, whilst at the same time, encourage them to make small steps towards independence. For example,

- ✔ Setting small timed tasks, using ways for the child to mark the time - an egg-timer, a watch with a clear face
- ✔ Gradually increasing the length and time needed for these tasks

- ✔ Letting the child know that you will get back to them and when that will be. You might say, for example, *"Try the first three questions on your own and then I will come back and check after X minutes"*.
- ✔ Make sure you do come back! - and if you get distracted, that you acknowledge what has happened. *"I am sorry I did not get back to when we agreed, that must have been worrying for you. You probably thought I had forgotten about you but you were still in my mind, it just took longer than I expected to get around to everyone else at the back"*. It is not necessary to be a 'perfect' teacher, keeping to your time frames exactly, but it is important to acknowledge the anxious feelings an unplanned delay can arouse in these children.
- ✔ Avoid the temptation to over-help. These pupils need to experience some frustration in order to develop their ability to problem-solve and learn. Rather than try to rescue or ignore their difficulty, you can acknowledge how frustrating learning like this can be. *"I know it feels impossible to do without the teacher next to you. It can feel very frustrating when we are learning something new. You can trust your brain to do it though"*. Over-helping can actually be counter-productive, leading these children to continue to rely on behaviour which can seem manipulative, but which perhaps, up to now, has been their only way of getting their needs met.

What worked with Jane?

The staff who taught Jane thought about her needs from an attachment perspective. They decided to use a consistent set of strategies in every lesson. In class they gave her specific time-limits for activities and also used a tick-list, where a teacher could tick at regular intervals that Jane was on task. This allowed them to acknowledge her in the class without distracting from the task. They asked one of the year 11 peer mentors to get Jane involved in lunchtime clubs on two afternoons.

Her form tutor agreed that Jane could come and help her on one lunchtime and that Jane could take responsibility for checking lunch tickets with a mid-day assistant on another day. Jane was also given a project with a group of peers in Geography and Maths which involved interviewing members of her year group and presenting the results to her class and teachers.

This gave her a chance to work with a group of peers and complete a task which brought her appropriately to the teacher's attention. In general teachers tried to give a name to Jane's feelings when she seemed to be anxious and attention-needy. For example, they said, "Jane, perhaps you are feeling anxious now and cannot bear waiting for me to come over, and if you wait five minutes, do these five questions, I will be back".

INSECURE AND AVOIDANT PATTERN

These children and young people have learned that if you seek attachment with someone, you will be rejected. Their response, perhaps not surprisingly, has been to avoid seeking attachment. They have experienced a caregiver who is not available physically or emotionally. Such unavailability may have arisen as a result of depression or feelings of not being able to cope with an infant. The caregiver may have been or become incapable of coping with her own emotions or of responding to her baby's needs. These children can then develop patterns of avoidant behaviour - a kind of *"I'll reject you before you reject me."* As they expect rebuff and rejection, they will not engage in relationships with adults which could expose them to this kind of rejection again.

How do we see this in class?

Bruce's silence

Bruce is also in year 8. He is considered to be high ability but to be underachieving. Like Jane he usually sits on his own, but not at the front of the class. He sits at the back, slouching, staring out of the window, and apparently paying no attention at all to what is going on around him. He does not look up when a teacher enters and seems pre-occupied, 'in a world of his own'. When she attempts to gain the attention of the class and start the lesson, he does not respond and continues to sit, gazing out of the window. Eventually, after his name has been called out three times for the register, he mumbles 'yes' and looks down at the table. The two boys sitting nearest him start laughing. The teacher can feel herself getting annoyed by this apparent disrespect and total lack of interest in her lesson.

Bruce is often sent out of class for not working and not responding to attempts to motivate him. His Head of Year says:

"I often have to try to talk to Bruce in the corridor when he has been sent out of a lesson. I can get nothing out of him. I try to be reasonable and understanding, encouraging him to give his version of events but he just stands there, silently, and shrugs his shoulders. I find it infuriating and often find myself shouting at him in frustration."

What could be happening with Bruce?

It appears that Bruce is exhibiting an insecure-avoidant attachment pattern. Bruce came from a chaotic family background. There were seven children in the family and Bruce's father left when Bruce was nine. Bruce's mother was suffering from depression and seemed unable to cope with parenting all these children. Bruce was the oldest boy and was often left to fend for himself, sometimes being picked up by the police and brought home late at night. He told his Head of Year that he went out of the house early in the morning and came back late at night so as "*not to get on his mum's nerves, 'coz she has enough to worry about.*" It seemed that for whatever reasons, Bruce's mum was finding it difficult to respond to Bruce's needs and he had responded by deciding to look after himself. In school, it meant that he could not trust other adults to help him.

Like Bruce, in class these children often -

→ show apparent indifference to the teacher
→ seem unable and unwilling to accept help, denying the need for support
→ say they don't care and shrug
→ seem unprepared to engage and discuss a problem
→ do not like the teacher to stand in close proximity
→ want to do tasks autonomously, even when they do not know what to do
→ show limited use of communication and creative opportunities, as this requires taking a risk with learning which they are not prepared to do
→ take refuge in the same kind of task and very quickly give up with any kind of new or more open-ended task
→ rip up their work, saying it is rubbish, before a teacher can comment on it It probably is not the standard they want, but would need input from the teacher to improve it and they cannot allow themselves to accept this

They may also present as the quiet child who does not say much but is noticeably underachieving. Girls in particular may tend to internalise their pain, possibly leading eventually to self-harm.

Insecure and avoidant pattern and the Learning Triangle

In the Learning Triangle (p.104) the focus for these children and young people is on the relationship between themselves and the task, and they reject the need for the child-adult relationship.

The task appears safe and they will seek refuge in it if they can, not being able to trust the relationship with the adult.

What does this behaviour pattern tell us about Bruce's needs?

Despite their apparent indifference, pupils such as Bruce are also very anxious. They can put themselves under a lot of pressure by not wanting to admit they need help. They may be at risk of developing compulsive behaviours as they have a strong need to feel they have an element of control over their world. These young people need to feel that they have some control of their situation and that they will not be rejected if they engage in a relationship with the teacher. They need to be allowed to feel safe with the task and then supported to move from engaging only with the task to gradually engaging with the relationship.

Teaching strategies

As with the previous pattern of insecure attachment, it is again important not to collude with their behaviour. Their overwhelming desire is to show you, the teacher, that they do not need the relationship with you. Often in schools, such children and young people refuse the help of a Teaching Assistant or teacher and seem very difficult to talk to, shutting down and not responding to well-meaning questions by people trying to help. They experience the relationship and questions as intrusive and dangerous. They can provoke extreme annoyance in staff, as we often feel that we really cannot 'teach' them or even discuss situations with them.

We feel helpless. At this stage, if we are not careful, the tendency is to ignore them or decide someone else needs to help them, not us. This is colluding with the pattern of rejection. So strategies need to be aimed at engaging with the pupil through the task. Through actions and discussions around the task, they can learn eventually to have a relationship with the teacher. It may be necessary to start with tasks which require minimal direct input from the teacher and through feedback on these tasks, allow the pupil to experience success in learning and move onto tasks which gradually allow more contact with the teacher.

- ✔ Allow them where possible some control and choice over their activities. This can often be built-in, for example, *"There are two practice tasks, you can choose to do them in the order you think is best"*
- ✔ Tasks are the key. Work through a task to develop a relationship around it. You can reach these children by commenting on the task itself rather than trying to build a relationship directly. For example, you might say *"That's an interesting idea. I was wondering how old that boy in the story is?",* rather than saying *"I'm really pleased with the ideas you've come up with, how about adding the age of the boy?".* The second sentence has an in-built implication that you, the teacher, have some part to play! The first comment stays in the metaphor of the task, the story
- ✔ Try to find tasks they enjoy doing and can be fairly self-directed on - this will allow them to get on with their work but, as the task and topic has been set by you, to have some connection to you as the teacher.
- ✔ Organise group and project work - children and young people displaying this pattern of aviodant behaviour may sometimes prefer to work with peers.
- ✔ Design tasks which involve a product rather than a process, for example, making a booklet, designing a poster, writing a newspaper article.

Avoidant children like to see achievable goals. They can share their product without obviously having to engage too much in the relationship. You can then move towards developing a relationship by discussing the finished product with them and using this thinking around the task to engage with them.

- ✔ The use of metaphor and story can be very successful with these students. Activities where they can draw, write or listen to stories, explore and discuss themes in books, on television, and in film, use drama or objects and so on will be initially safer than those which ask them to speak directly about themselves. The teacher can then discuss the characters in the stories or comment on the drawings and draw them into the relationship gradually.
- ✔ Left-brain, concrete, mechanical tasks such as sorting, organising, categorizing, building, clearing up - are all ways these pupils can be involved in the daily routine of the class. They can help the class and teacher with a task such a wiping the board without acknowledging that they are doing it to improve their relationships!
- ✔ Work with other staff to ensure a consistent, positive approach which does not result in further rejection of the child.

What worked with Bruce?

When I had Bruce in my French class I tried to set him up with an independent activity as soon as possible during the lesson. I told him that it was okay not to join in verbally, but that I would give him a task which allowed him to show what he knew. He enjoyed doing worksheets on which he could check his answers on his own. I gave him a tape to listen to so that he could then make his own recording on the topic.

I said I trusted him to keep to the deadlines. If I saw he was struggling I tried to incorporate his difficulties into the lesson, saying I had noticed a few people were still not sure about the task, or I created a revision worksheet which focused on some of the mistakes I had noticed him making. I asked another boy to sit next to Bruce so that they could 'help each other'. I tried to develop his ability to accept help by quietly indicating when he had done something well or rewarding his whole group for successful tasks.

On some days, it was a struggle to keep him in class as his apparent indifference felt very much like an attack on me but I tried to resist the temptation to make him work somewhere else on his own. At times, he was like a little island in the middle of the class.

With children like this it is difficult to assess if you are making progress. At the extreme end, they might not want to talk to you at all. A breakthrough for me was when Bruce came in at the time of the football World Cup, holding out a card with the Irish flag carefully coloured on the front, saying 'For Miss Delaney'. *"How nice!"* I thought, and then opened it up to read 'You lost!'. I laughed and enjoyed the joke. I could have chosen to see this as an attack, but I felt it was his way of acknowledging that we had a relationship. Children whose behaviour follows these patterns are never going to come up to you and say *"Thanks a lot for helping me Miss"*. You will however, sometimes be fortunate enough to observe positive developments in other ways!

INSECURE AND DISORGANISED PATTERN

These children come from chaotic, damaged backgrounds, usually suffering severe neglect, violence and/or abuse. They seem erratic in their responses and can display very distressing behaviours which put them or others at risk, for example, smashing their fists against walls until they draw blood when frustrated or after being corrected. It is not always possible to see the immediate trigger to their extreme behaviour. They are very difficult to teach and the most challenging to respond to, but fortunately constitute the smallest percentage of pupils in the insecure attachment group. They often develop controlling/punitive behaviour towards the parent and other adults. They have very impoverished relationships, even with their peers.

How do we see this in class?

Matthew's turmoil

Matthew was an eleven year old in year 7 of secondary school. He had a history of non-attendance in primary school and when he was in school was often sent out of or ran out of class. Sometimes he had been sent home and sometimes he would sit outside the Headteacher's office, drawing and colouring in as he would not attempt any age-appropriate work.

*Matthew seemed totally unmanageable in secondary school. He ran out of lessons, running away from staff, hitting other children in the playground and rarely sat still long enough to discuss anything with staff who were trying to help him. In meetings with his mother and stepfather they often expressed the desire for him to be taken away to 'boarding school'. At this point Matthew would show remorse, cry and beg to be given another chance. He used to run in and out of the Learning Support Unit, shouting "You can't f***ing help me, I won't come in here". Each time he did this, the staff told him that he was welcome any time and did not even have to talk to us if he did not want to.*

Some of the other children tried to get him to stay and work with them.

What could be happening with Matthew?

Matthew appears to be exhibiting an insecure-disorganised attachment pattern. He had a fragmented family history. His mother had given birth to seven children but only three of them lived with her and her new partner. The other four lived with their birth fathers. Matthew was the oldest child living at home and his mother often said that the only reason she had kept him was because his birth father did not want him. Matthew had attended several primary schools as his mother had moved several times. He had arrived at his last primary school in year 6 and had spent much of his time sitting outside the Headteacher's office or on a part-time timetable, where he only attended school in the mornings. He had never been assessed by an Educational Psychologist as his mother had said he did not have special needs, he just needed discipline. At one point she admitted that she had been in a special, residential school as a child, and found it difficult to deal with teachers.

Children and young people with this pattern of erratic responses and distressing behaviours can disrupt lessons and cause upset to the teacher and other pupils. They can often -

→ change rapidly from being very agitated to 'switched off'.
One minute they might be loudly demanding your attention,
and the next, telling you they do not need you and to go away
→ get very frustrated and show this by banging their heads
against the wall
→ run around uncontrollably
→ run out of class unexpectedly
→ explode into temper for no apparent reason
→ be very abusive to the other children in the class
→ be very abusive to the teacher, rubbishing their attempts to teach

It is difficult to plan for these children, as they may respond differently from week to week. They expect the worse - and indeed, it has usually happened - and cannot believe that anyone will care about them consistently. They are, in fact, focused on survival. They have a constant need to be hyper-vigilant and look for dangers, real and imagined. It can help to remember that much of their difficult behaviour is prompted by fear and overwhelming anxiety. They quite simply have no space in their minds to think or engage in relationships. Working with the family can also be difficult, as it may be unlikely that the parents will engage with the necessary support services.

Insecure and disorganised pattern and the Learning Triangle

These pupils are not engaging in any section of the Learning Triangle: I often feel that they are floating above it or around it. These are the children and young people we will feel most helpless about. We need to be careful that our own feelings of helplessness do not turn into punitive approaches, reacting angrily to these children's destructive behaviour because we feel completely useless in our attempts to help.

What does this behaviour pattern tell us about Matthew's needs?

It is difficult to plan for the needs of pupils such as Matthew, as they may respond differently from week to week. They expect catastrophes to occur at any moment - as indeed, outside school, they often have. They cannot trust adults to care for them. They live in constant fear and anxiety. They need, therefore, to have a strong, containing structure which can withstand their overwhelming, painful feelings and enable them to feel SAFE. They need to know that there is a structure to school and learning, which they may eventually learn to rely on. They may have experienced ridicule, humiliation and denigration from adults, and will need to be shown that this will not be the case in school.

Teaching strategies

- ✔ Provide emotional containment for the staff. The key task in working with these children and young people is to acknowledge the strain put on us by their chaotic behaviour. When working with them, we can experience high levels of anxiety as we cannot be sure how they will react on a daily basis. Unexpected eruptions, aggression, persistent refusal to co-operate or focus on the lesson, an apparent lack of respect and empathy towards others are wearying experiences on a daily basis, and attack the thinking capacity of the teacher. We need to see our task as maintaining and restoring our own capacity to think, and subsequently, the child's.

Working with these children therefore requires a strong network, regular meetings, and discussions with other professionals dealing with this pupil. These meetings should not be called only in emergencies and as a reaction to an incident, but be set up as an on-going reflective process. We need to avoid the examples of splitting and blaming described in previous chapters. We need to provide the strong 'container' for our emotions, in order to allow thought.

- ✔ Have a strong support group for yourself,
- ✔ Have a routine and structure
- ✔ Use visual timetables if appropriate to show the daily routines
- ✔ Flag up any changes to routine in advance if possible, reflect back how catastrophic a change might feel
- ✔ If there are going to be many changes in the day, for example the arrival of supply teachers, think about allowing this child to work somewhere

safe with a trusted adult

- ✔ If that is not possible, have a back-up plan in case the child or young person erupts in class or give them a timeout card to use. They may need, for example, to have a safe place to go to, where they can do simple worksheets and calm down.
- ✔ Transitions and endings need to be carefully planned and acknowledged (*see* Chapter 9 *on transitions*).
- ✔ If possible, in class, allow them to sit near the teacher and near the door so that they can indicate if they need help and need to escape
- ✔ Make use of logical, left-brain, concrete tasks such as sorting, ordering, categorising, filling in and colouring in. These tasks will soothe their anxiety and provide some kind of logical order. Tasks which involve metaphorical thinking and creativity may be quite frightening for these children.
- ✔ These children quite literally need to be 'found' and brought back. Make use of activities which involve finding a missing link, putting something back into the picture, completing a puzzle, joining the dots and so on.
- ✔ Take a small step-by-step approach. Find something they are good at and allow them to spend some time on this when they are out of other classes. This needs to be part of an agreed plan. It is not a 'reward' for bad behaviour, but an acknowledgement that they are still a capable person even when they have been unable to manage themselves in the classroom.
- ✔ Acknowledge how difficult it might be to stay in class and trust their ability to learn.

What worked with Matthew?

Matthew's form tutor and Head of Year worked hard to help Matthew. In meetings with his parents, they reiterated their desire to work with Matthew and to see his good points. He was bright, very good at maths and had been noticed by some staff being kind to other younger children. His maths teacher kept him near the front of the class, near the door, and encouraged him to do extra worksheets if he finished or had missed some work by his non-attendance. The Learning Support Manager kept appointments free for Matthew, even if he would not come in to the unit and just ran around outside. Eventually he began to go into the Learning Support Unit and stand in the corner, refusing to engage in work but watching what was going on.

The Head of Year held a lunchtime meeting of all the staff who taught Matthew, in order to discuss a consistent approach to him when he did appear in class. It was agreed that he

- *could sit near the door in every class*
- *have extra worksheets to do on his own if agitated*
- *could take the role of the observer where possible, for example, filming the class in Drama*
- *would agree - a signal when he needed to leave the room, the place he would go, and how long he would spend there*

All of these strategies were designed to give Matthew clear boundaries but to allow him some flexibility when his anxiety overwhelmed his ability to stay in class and learn. By having an agreed plan, staff were able to keep some control of the situation but to acknowledge Matthew's fragile sense of self as a learner. The Head of Year kept a 'Find Wally' book in her office which he often needed to go and look at. It seemed the task of finding Wally in chaotic, busy environments helped him calm down and find a place for himself.

It was never easy, and there were times he was excluded for complete non-co-operation. Eventually Matthew transferred to a Pupil Referral Unit to complete his schooling. The staff at his mainstream school felt, however, that they were able to share valuable information and insight with the Unit, and he did complete some exams successfully.

PAUSE FOR THOUGHT

Think about the children you teach

Do any of them display behaviour patterns that might match the groups described above?

If you describe their behaviour as communicating their needs in this way, how might that affect your thinking about them ?

What teaching strategies could you then develop to meet these needs?

CONTAINMENT

Bion (1961, 1970) writes about the need for the adult to provide 'containment' of the overwhelming feelings an infant might have. As discussed previously, a school can be full of powerful feelings which can threaten to overwhelm us, particularly around the behaviour of certain children. It can be difficult to acknowledge when we are feeling overwhelmed as we feel we should be able to cope, that we need to be 'strong' in order to set a good example. We do need to be able to manage these feelings but that is not the same as ignoring and suppressing them. If feelings are suppressed or ignored, in an attempt to appear 'strong' and able to cope, they will often come to the surface in some other way, in stress-related illnesses for example - a key reason for teachers leaving the profession.

We need to be able to recognise the feelings, digest them, and think about them without panicking. It is not just the children's feelings which need to be contained, but also our own. This is why support groups are so important.

Before thinking about emotional containment, however, it is important to realise that the school building itself needs to provide containment for some children, particularly those with an avoidant or disorganised attachment pattern of behaviour, before relationships can begin to develop.

The school building can come to represent a secure physical base. It is a place where

→ rules and boundaries are clear
→ routines are established
→ in general, the day is predictable
→ the roles of adult and child are clear

As I said in my introduction, even if these children seem to hate the rules and kick against them, they are looking, however unconsciously, to be 'contained'.

In fact, for many children, school is the safest place to act out and protest. The boundaries in school may seem safer and stronger than at home, and therefore need to be tested and to stick. In Margot Sunderland's story *'Willy and the Wobbly House'* (from the *'Helping Children with Feelings'* series, Speechmark Publishing, 2001) a boy called Willy lives in a house where everything wobbles. His friend Joe next door lives in a house with only straight lines. Both prefer the other's house. Many children live in these types of wobbly houses or within severe lines, and the school building can come to represent a place which is neither wobbly nor rigid, but can be flexible as well as firm.

Examples of containment

Liam was a thirteen year old who was violent at home and not at school. When I asked him why he was able to work at school, he said the rules were clearer.

Sandra was continually aggressive in school. Having started to make a relationship with her, and having an understanding of what was going on for her outside school, I commented that sometimes school is the safest place to vent anger that cannot be safely contained outside school. She agreed, and, over time, learned to express her hurt feelings more.

As a teacher, this can be very hard to accept. You might be the very person who is trying the hardest to work with a particular pupil, yet you will be the one most 'punished' by their behaviour. Try to see what happens as a sign that you are the key attachment figure and you are being 'tested' to see if you can contain the emotions. Sometimes this can be very difficult. If you are the person who has worked most closely to support a child, it can feel almost unfathomable when they seem to turn against you.

Containing Shannon's feelings

Shannon was a fifteen year old girl who had been self-harming and saying she wanted to kill herself. She had formed a close relationship with her Head of Year who had been meeting her regularly to allow her to talk through her feelings. Shannon's behaviour in class began to get worse, and she started truanting classes, saying she was going to see her Head of Year. The Head of Year had to discuss this with Shannon and say that she would refuse to see her if she kept truanting lessons. Shannon got very upset and wrote a letter to the teacher, telling her she hated her and that she had told her Mum that no-one in the school had tried to help her. The Head of Year was very upset, as she felt she had given up a lot of her time trying to help and that it was a very unfair accusation. She told the Head that she thought the girl's behaviour was out-of-control and could not be contained in the school.

This was an unfortunate example of a member of staff who needed support to process what was going on for her and this girl in the relationship. The rejection she felt, although understandable, caused her to disengage and become quite persecutory, mirroring the girl's behaviour.

PAUSE FOR THOUGHT

Read the example of Shannon again. Think about the emotional needs of the Head of Year

What might have helped the Head of Year in her dealings with Shannon?

How could the school or colleagues have provided this support for her?

In summary

Attachment theory as developed by John Bowlby and Mary Ainsworth, can be a useful model for thinking about the needs of seemingly unteachable children and young people.

- Infants are pre-programmed to develop attachment behaviour and use this attachment as a secure base from which to develop and explore
- Children with an early secure attachment experience can readily develop skills for learning. Their relationship to the teacher and to tasks is in balance
- Children with insecure attachment experiences may be unable to learn, as they are too pre-occupied with checking out their relationship with the teacher or they will only focus on the task and not allow help. The Learning Triangle between pupil/teacher and task is skewed in some way.
- Teachers often come to represent key attachment figures in these children's lives
- Before thinking about strategies to manage these children, we need to think about their underlying needs and the experiences they have not had
- Don't collude with their patterns of behaviour. For example, if they exhibit an avoidant pattern, make every effort not to reject them or to be 'over-bright' in your dealing with them

- Children with an ambivalent-resistant insecure attachment need to learn to separate from the adult in small steps and to pay attention to the task

- Children with an avoidant insecure attachment need to learn to trust the relationship with an adult, but through engagement with a task

- Children with a disorganised attachment style are the most chaotic and difficult to teach. However, they represent a small percentage of 'unteachable' children and young people. For them, it is imperative we develop and work with a strong network and clear, consistent routines

- Schools can provide the experience of what Bion called the 'containment' of potentially overwhelming feelings for these children - both emotionally, through routines and relationships, and physically, through the buildings

- At school children have the opportunity to experience new ways of relating which offer a 'second-chance' at developing secure attachment patterns

- Children will sometimes turn against the adult who has supported them most. This is a testing of the relationship and its boundaries. It should not be seen as rejection; the adult needs to resist the desire to give up working with the pupil, and find appropriate support for him or herself.

Chapter 8

How learning to play impacts in the classroom

D. W. Winnicott was a pædiatrician and child psychoanalyst who looked at how children learn to play. He was interested in how the development of play allows the development of the child's identity and ability to have relationships. His theories on play and observation of children give us another way of looking at some of our pupils' behaviour. In this chapter I will be giving a brief overview, in Winnicott's terms, of the stages a child goes through when learning to play and linking these with the play skills needed to be a good learner in the classroom. I will also be looking at Winnicott's theories on the value of observation without interpretation, and how this can be a useful skill for teachers to develop and practise in the classroom.

Winnicott believed that through interaction with the mother and play, the baby and young child learn to have a sense of '*me and not-me*'. By developing this sense of separateness, the child can learn to play in a space which is between the two. This is the space in which learning can take place. If we consider for a moment how a young child learns to play, we can recognise the developmental stages cited by Winnicott (1971):

→ Playing with the mother, not separately
→ Playing with self, toes, fingers and so on
→ Playing with an object, for example, a blanket, a soft toy
→ Playing alone, but in the mother's presence
→ Playing alongside another child (a stage often seen in nursery school,

where two children will be playing, for example, in the 'home' area, but not with each other, alongside each other)

→ Inviting another child to join in your play
→ Being invited in to play another child's game and being able to follow their rules and inventions

WHAT STAGE OF PLAY HAVE THE 'UNTEACHABLE' CHILDREN REACHED ?

If we use this concept to look at the behaviour of some of those struggling in our classes, we can see that there is an assumption that children, in order to learn in a classroom environment, have reached the final stage of play development. In effect, they need to be able to play by someone else's rules - be it the teacher's, the school's, or society's in general. Many of the pupils I deal with are those who - even in secondary - have not reached this stage of play. They cheat if they are not winning, they cannot wait for a turn, they cannot bear to lose and they argue about rules if they cannot follow them.

Terry's cheating

Terry, fifteen, was in foster care. He had been in several foster placements in the early years of his life and had not stayed anywhere long enough to develop many social skills. He found it very difficult to settle in most of his classes. He found it particularly difficult to work in groups with other pupils. He initially enjoyed group tasks with an element of competition, but would inevitably cheat or spoil things by shouting out the answer in guessing games such as Pictionary if his group was not winning. Other pupils were very frustrated with him and usually refused to work with him. Teachers found him frustrating to deal with as he was continually arguing about rules and instructions. His Geography teacher said "All I ever hear from Terry is "Well, yesterday you told us a different way to do this" or ..."That's not how our other teacher does it". If he can't do something, it is always because the instruction or rule was wrong. It drives me mad. I feel like I am dealing with the tantrums of a four year old"

Teaching implications

It seems that Terry may not have learned some basic play skills when younger. Pupils like Terry may demonstrate this by:

→ being unable to take turns in class or in their group

→ spoiling things for others, for example by cheating, when they are not winning

→ insisting on going first in games and sulking or getting angry if they are not picked

→ trying to take over in group work with their peers and not listening to other people's ideas

→ refusing to participate if their group overrides their decisions or does not choose their ideas

→ arguing about rules and instructions and then trying to change them if they are losing or getting something wrong, saying, for example, "*Well, when I've done this before, we didn't do it like this*"

This can be incredibly frustrating for a teacher, as it can feel like you are dealing with a much younger pupil. We might feel that the young person is "*doing it deliberately"* if he or she is an older student, and react in an angry, punitive way, telling the pupil to *"grow up and stop being such a baby"*. In fact, they may well be acting in the only way they know. They have not developed the social skills to deal with being in a group and following the group rules. They may well feel shame and humiliation when they lose a game or cannot follow a rule. This shame might be covered up by angry outbursts and arguments in which they pretend they are playing by different rules - hence the continual comments such as "*We did it a different way the last time*". They cannot bear the humiliation of losing.

These children and young people also find it hard to make friends, as other pupils do not want to work with them and will either react angrily to their behaviour or simply avoid their company. Eventually this will lead them to be isolated and probably even more disaffected.

Learning takes place in the space between the adult and the child. Our first experience of separateness and use of this space is through learning to play as a young child. If a pupil has missed out on this, we need to provide opportunities to develop these skills - no matter what age the child or young person is. In my experience, the need for these skills to be nurtured and taught is more easily recognised in lower primary, but we also need to realise that there are many children coming into secondary school who still haven't acquired them. These students need to experience what educational psychotherapists call 'second-chance learning.'

Winnicott (1971) says that the therapist's work -

> ...is directed towards bringing the patient from a state of not being able to play into a state of being able to play. (p.36)

The parallel for us as teachers is '*how do we get our students into a state of being able to learn and able to make use of that transitional space'*. For some pupils, this will entail learning to play. The use of games in the classroom, therefore, can have a wider and more far-reaching effect that we might imagine.

USING GAMES

Any opportunity you can find to include play and games in your classroom will help children develop skills that make learning possible. Even if we accept the connection between developing play skills and learning skills, we can feel guilty when we play games in the classroom, worrying that it is perhaps a waste of time or not a legitimate part of formal learning. There is no need to feel guilty if it is a well-thought out game. For example, I would often play a game called 'Backs to the Board' with my French classes. In this game, one person has their back to the board and the other has to give them the French translation of a word I write on the board. This revises vocabulary, but equally importantly it involves co-operation, listening and teamwork.

You can use competitive games such as 'Connect Four' and chess as rewards, but exploit them fully by asking students what other skills they are developing. These kinds of games develop the important skills of empathy. In order to play chess and 'Connect Four' it is necessary to think of your own moves, but also be aware of the possible moves of your partner. The best players stay one step ahead and try to predict their partner's strategies as well as their own. Being able to pay attention to yourself and another person, to recognise what is required by the teacher and other pupils, are vital skills for learning to take place in a classroom. There are a wealth of Circle Time games which can be used in this way as well.

Moreover, games can be used which allow children and young people to express hostile feelings in a safe way, an important experience for children who have not had their feelings contained. For example, a competitive game such as hangman may be helpful for a child whose hostility towards being taught is blocking their capacity to learn. It can allow the child to defeat the teacher *through* learning rather than through not learning. Battleships, dominoes, and pelmanism are all examples of games which fulfill this purpose, and can be used for revision and learning.

(For more of these kinds of games, see pp.xxx: see also Rinvolucri & Davis 1990, Hadfield 1992 and Mosley 1996)

THE TRANSITIONAL SPACE - A LINK WITH READING

Learning takes place in the space between the adult and the child - in what Winnicott calls the *transitional space*, the space where fantasy is tested against reality. If you watch a young child playing with their cars or bricks, developing stories and creating fantasy worlds, you will see that they are bringing in learning from reality and applying it within their own internal worlds. Moreover, in play, one thing can represent another in the same way that reading and writing are representations of reality. Consequently, if children can understand and take part in symbolic play, they are more likely to be better placed to be able to learn to read and write. Through play, the young child learns disillusionment and to bear frustration, both of which are vital in our ability to learn. There is an explicit link between learning and play. Some children who seem unable to learn to read have not actually learned the value of symbolic play, such as drama games, mime, matching symbols to meaning and imaginative stories.

Sarah's secret skill

Sarah was in year 5 of primary and her classteacher, Ms Nash, was very concerned about her reading ability.

"I find it impossible to assess Sarah's reading level. Most of the time, she appears to recognise very few words and performs very badly in reading tests. However, in class, I sometimes catch her doing an activity which requires understanding some written instructions. Also, her mother tells me that sometimes she shows she can read road signs, for example, when they have taken a wrong turning and Sarah points it out. I really don't know what is going on with her".

Ms Nash learned something about Winnicott's theories of play and thought that Sarah had perhaps not learned how to play at a younger age. She began to include more competitive games such as hangman and word battleships and to sometimes ask Sarah to demonstrate the game to the rest of the class. Sarah seemed to enjoy this, although she found it difficult when she lost. Ms Nash said at these times "It feels as if you cannot bear to lose". Sarah did not respond immediately but on one occasion when she beat Ms Nash, said "Wow, you know a lot but you don't know everything". Ms Nash also encouraged the class, including Sarah, to bring in some of their favourite card games and teach the others the rules. At first Sarah used to change the rules in her game if she was losing but Ms Nash always tried to comment on how difficult it can be to lose and that rules can be hard to follow at times.

Eventually Sarah began to show in class that she could read quite well for her age and allowed herself to be taught new words. It seems that the games helped her in two ways. By practising playing and learning to win and lose, she was able to accept the classroom rules and the pain of not always getting it right. In addition, some of the more imaginative games allowed her explore how one thing might represent another. For example, she enjoyed games such as 'Guess what my object is'. In this game, pupils pass an imaginary object around the class and take turns to do a mime with it, turning it into something new each time. Games such as these allow pupils such as Sarah to defeat the teacher and her peers in a safe way. She no longer had to defeat the adults by not learning.

OBSERVATION SKILLS

Another key part of Winnicott's work, and also that of the child psychoanalyst, Anna Freud, was their detailed observation of children at play. They both emphasised the need to observe and *not* make immediate interpretations. Anna Freud believed that the first step in understanding children was 'careful, detailed and open-minded observation' and that this should be followed only later by 'theoretical conceptualisation' (Edgcumbe, 2000, p.7). Winnicott also stated:

> I withhold interpretations, and often make no sound at all... My reward for withholding interpretations comes when the patient makes the interpretation herself. (Winnicott, 1971, p.57)

How can we, as teachers, take opportunities to develop this kind of skill and what use does it have? Essentially, it should enable us to create a space in which to think about the children and young people we find most difficult to teach. As teachers, we can practise noticing something about a child and commenting on it, or picking up on a feeling and trying to name it. Winnicott says that by naming the feelings, we allow 'fantasy to be checked with reality', and increase the 'capacity to remember' (Winnicott 1971). He does not see not being able to interpret *the meaning* of a behaviour as a failure.

I have found this a very useful concept to bear in mind when trying to make sense of some children's behaviour. As classroom teachers, we need to try to notice the key features and feelings without worrying immediately what to do about them. We need to give ourselves the freedom and space to think about and acknowledge what we see and feel, without a sense of urgency pushing us to jump to conclusions. If we can name what we observe, we can discuss what it means to the child rather than our interpretation of it. Ultimately we might get further with getting the child to change their behaviour.

Jack's graffiti

Jack was in trouble in school for drawing graffiti on his desk and on walls around the school. Most staff in the school were very annoyed and thought this was a sign of disrespect for them and the school building.

His Head of Year, Mr Thomas, was fed up with the situation and had tried several ways of dealing with the problem, including discussing consequences, fixed-term exclusions and reporting Jack to the police. He was not convinced of the value of 'just' stating what he observed but he decided to try it as a last resort: he felt he had nothing to lose and could at least say he had tried everything before Jack was permanently excluded.

He tried to describe Jack's behaviour in a simple way, by observing what he had noticed about it. The Head of Year said to Jack, "I've noticed that you don't always do the same type of graffiti. It appears to be in different styles. I was wondering why that is."

Jack was taken aback. He had not expected this. He told Mr Thomas that he was experimenting with different styles because he was setting up a business, offering to customize cars, rooms and other personal possessions for people. Mr Thomas was amazed; he would not have thought that Jack had the initiative to think like this. He asked Jack to think of a way to practice his graffiti and business skills without breaking school rules and upsetting people. Jack suggested that he provide graffiti signs for subject teachers who agreed. The Head of Year asked him to submit a business proposal including the costing and time commitment and to address it to the Headteacher. Jack did this, and after some negotiation was able to provide some classroom signs, as well as use the work for his Business Studies GCSE assignment.

Mr Thomas commented, "I was amazed what I found out about Jack, when I stopped interpreting and judging his behaviour and just tried to describe what I observed. We ended up with a positive result for all of us, something which was not happening in our other attempts to stop Jack. I am sure that we would eventually have excluded him permanently if we had continued to assume his motives were bad. To tell the truth, I was initially quite cynical about this approach and, if I had not seen it with my own eyes, would never have believed such a simple thing would affect such a big change"

PAUSE FOR THOUGHT

Think about a student you find difficult to teach

Observe what they are doing and saying.

Describe the behaviour you have noticed.

Make sure you have not included a lot of judgements. For example, *"Susan doesn't listen"* is not a description, but a judgement. It does not tell me what Susan is doing to make you think she does not listen.

Try describing the behaviour in a non-judgemental way the next time you deal with the child and say you find it interesting. What do you find out that is new and different? What new strategies can you develop from this?

AND OF COURSE IT CAN BE FUN

Let's not forget that, above all, playing should be fun. Children who learn to play at an early age learn to have fun with their parent/carer and to take delight in the relationship. The parent/carer also gets great enjoyment out of playing with their child. If we can allow ourselves to play and have fun in our classes, we are showing our pupils that learning can be fun, that a relationship with an adult in school can sometimes be light-hearted and playful. Many of our 'unteachable' pupils will not have had this experience. Moreover, it gives us an opportunity to see our pupils in a different light. This can be particularly important with those pupils with whom we are constantly in conflict. By relating to them in a more relaxed way, perhaps through a game or play activity, we might be able to enjoy their personality, acknowledge their sense of humour and find it easier to give them geniunely positive attention.

In summary

DW Winnicott's understanding of how children learn to play can influence our thoughts about learning and those children and young people who cannot seem to learn in our classes.

- Children in trouble at school have often not negotiated the stages of play successfully. In particular, they have not developed the ability to play by someone else's rules

- Children need to have experience of the transitional space, the space between the adult and the child where play takes place. This space allows them to learn, testing their own internal fantasy world against the external reality. It is an essential step in their development of a self as a separate being from the adult

- Tasks and games can be designed for our classes to help these children learn to play and express their feelings in a safe way

- Games and tasks can give a child a chance to express hostile feelings towards the teacher and learning. Games offer the opportunity to 'defeat' the teacher by learning, rather than by 'not-learning'

- Through guessing, competitive and turn-taking games, the child can learn to bear not knowing an answer and feeling frustrated - key skills in learning

- Playing is therefore not a waste of time - even in secondary, there are children who have not yet reached the final stage of being able to play
- Our job is to get pupils into a state of readiness for learning, and this may be through play and games
- It is important for teachers to develop the skill of noticing what is happening and maybe naming it, rather than jumping into an interpretation of what it might mean. We need to think with the child about the possible meanings of their behaviour
- Learning can be fun. The use of play and games in lessons can give both the teacher and the pupils a chance to be part of an enjoyable, positive learning environment

Chapter 9

Beginnings, transitions and endings

WHY THEY ARE DIFFICULT

For many children experiencing problems at school, beginnings of new school years and new terms, transitions from one class to another, changes of teacher, movement from primary to secondary, can all be very traumatic. You may have noticed that children with behavioural problems often don't come into school at the end of term, or behave so badly that they are excluded for the final days. Many staff think that this is because they are just happy to be breaking up. In fact the opposite may be true. Endings and transitions bring back memories of other endings of relationships, relationships suddenly being disrupted, loved ones going away, things not being the same.

Transitions involve loss and dealing with uncertainty. They can trigger powerful and negative feelings, particularly if a child or young person has not successfully negotiated the psychological stages of permanency and constancy. I will briefly describe these stages here and how they relate to pupil behaviour in school *(for a more in-depth explanation of these terms and their effect on transitions, see* Bomber 2007, pp. 159-183).

PERMANENCY

Permanency is the term given to the psychological developmental milestone children reach when they realise that objects and people exist and will continue to exist, even when they cannot be seen or are in their immediate vicinity. The child has learnt to understand that he himself will continue to exist when not being seen or directly connected to by the adult. Put simply, the child can understand that an adult who has left the room, or even the home, will continue to exist and will remember the child and keep them in mind. The child realises that he or she exists as a separate person and can do so without constant contact with the adult.

This sense of self as a separate being comes from the child having repeated, consistent and sensitive care-giving experiences. A child who has lived with trauma, abuse and loss, however, may not have had this experience. This child will need to seek constant reassurance that the adult, when she is absent for some time, will be able to remember him and think about him. So an ending or a transition may bring up feelings of abandonment and vulnerability for a child who has not passed through this stage. It will be impossible for him to believe that the teacher will remember him when he moves on to a new class, or that the experiences they had together were in any way meaningful.

Katie's problem with transitions

Katie is a year 9 pupil who has formed a strong bond with her Head of Year, Ms Walsh. Katie struggled in the transition to secondary school, and Miss Walsh gave her a lot of individual time, listening to her feelings and setting her up with a peer mentor to help her settle. Ms Walsh has moved with Katie through years 7-9. Katie did well in her year 9 SATs exams and up until recently, had seemed to be progressing well. In year 10 she will have a new Head of Year as she will be moving into upper school.

In the spring term of year 9, the pupils were given their information booklets about GCSE choices. There were several information meetings for parents and pupils about the Key Stage 4 curriculum. Katie did not attend any of them. She did not complete her options choices and she did not turn up for scheduled meetings with her form tutor to discuss them. When her form tutor spoke to her parents, they said that Katie kept saying she would look at the booklet later, and then that she had left it in school or lost it.

Katie has also begun to disrupt classes and is constantly being sent to Ms Walsh, whom she refuses to speak to. Ms Walsh is upset about this as she has always felt that she had a good relationship with Katie. Now she says, "I can't seem to get through to Katie any more. She has never been an easy pupil to deal with, but I really felt that she trusted me to help now. Now it feels as if it was all a waste of time and we are back at the beginning."

What could be happening with Katie ?

We can see that Katie is having great difficulty in the transition from Key Stage 3 to Key Stage 4. She has benefited from a strong relationship with her Head of Year and discussions about moving on are bringing up feelings of abandonment and fear of not surviving on her own. It is interesting that Katie also found the transition from primary to secondary difficult. It suggests that perhaps she had some problems progressing through the permanency stage of development. We cannot always know the background of the children we teach, but, in cases such as Katie's, we can notice repeated examples of a problem which might give us some insight into what is going on. In this example, there definitely seems to be a repeated pattern of problematic transitions.

What can we do for Katie?

It is essential that Katie is helped to understand that transitions do not have to be traumatic and that an adult can remember her and think about her when she has moved on. It was important in Katie's case that the Head of Year 9 spent some time with her and was able to acknowledge how painful transitions can be. Time would need to be spent on naming the range of feelings Katie might be experiencing, such as anger, disappointment and fear. Ms Walsh could help Katie to realise that these seemingly overwhelming feelings are completely normal and valid feelings in this situation. (*See below for more ideas on marking these kinds of transitions, p.149*)

CONSTANCY

Constancy is the psychological developmental milestone by which children are able to perceive themselves and their carers as integrated whole beings. They have come to understand that their parent or carer remains consistently the same person even though they may show different sides to their personality. For example, an adult can sometimes be irritated with a child, but also, at other times, the same adult can be very patient. A parent can be happy and sad, proud and disappointed. Children learn that the parent is not all bad or all good, that this is just part of who they are and that this is acceptable and normal. Children who realise this can then allow these kinds of feelings in themselves. If they make a mistake, they do not carry around the feeling that they are a completely 'bad' person. They can begin to understand, for example, that you can feel angry at a person for leaving and, at the same time, be sad because you will miss them.

These type of conflicting feelings - happiness at moving on and sadness at what is being left behind - are an integral part of any transition or ending. If a child has successfully learned this in their early years, they will find transitions at school easier to cope with. For those who have not, the conflicting feelings can be confusing and frightening. They can begin to think that they must be a 'bad' person to have such feelings.

Jimmy and Mr Crowley

Jimmy is in year 6 and after a difficult start in Reception class, where he often did not want to stay in school, has really enjoyed primary school. In the last two years he has been taught by the same teacher, Mr Crowley, who has encouraged his interests in sport and music. Jimmy has often said that he feels Mr Crowley is his friend and understands him. He has told Mr Crowley that he does not ever want to leave his class and that he would never stay in school if Mr Crowley left.

Mr Crowley feels uncomfortable when Jimmy makes these comments and tries to reassure him, saying: "Of course you would Jimmy, there are lots of people here to help you, you really don't just need me."

Still, Mr Crowley is not sure this is the right thing to say as it does not seem to convince Jimmy. Mr Crowley is aware that the transition from primary to secondary will be difficult for Jimmy and he has arranged for a Learning Mentor from the secondary school to liaise with teachers and the Learning Mentors at the primary. However, Mr Crowley is now finding Jimmy increasingly difficult to manage. He is continually shouting out in class, taking other children's equipment and then bursting into tears when the teacher tries to talk to him about his behaviour. He often shouts angrily that he hates Mr Crowley, that he has changed, doesn't care about him any more and he (Jimmy) will be glad to leave his stupid class. Very often, Jimmy then becomes very remorseful and says he was sorry, he is a bad person and Mr Crowley should leave him alone, he doesn't deserve help.

What could be happening with Jimmy?

This is a very distressing time for Jimmy and his teacher. Jimmy appears to be struggling with very strong emotions - he hates his teacher for allowing him to move on but feels great affection for him as a result of the relationship they built up together in primary. These are completely acceptable and normal emotions, but Jimmy has not learned that it is normal to have these conflicting feelings in an important transition. He would appear to believe that he is 'bad' for having the 'bad' feelings towards the teacher he really likes. Again, without knowing much about Jimmy's early years, it is interesting that he found the beginning of school life difficult and is now finding the transition from primary to secondary traumatic.

What can we do for Jimmy?

As previously seen with Katie, it is important that Jimmy's teacher spends some time helping him to understand these powerful and overwhelming feelings. First, however, Mr Crowley needs to be able to process his own feelings and thoughts on the matter, as he is also experiencing strong emotions, possibly guilt and anxiety about not being able to help Jimmy and fear that Jimmy actually might not do well in school without his help. We can see how the ideas of *projection* and *transference*, described in Chapter 6, may be affecting the teacher's thinking here.

It is important to show Jimmy that it is okay to have these different feelings and that we all have many different parts to us. Mr Crowley could tell Jimmy that we can like someone and be angry with them at the same time. He will need to work with the Learning Mentors to support Jimmy in his transition, but also give him ways to acknowledge and remember the work he has done with him. For example, he might make a memory book about his time in Mr Crowley's class, and Mr Crowley could also contribute some ideas.

So, we have seen that children who have little history of trusting relationships, but who have nevertheless formed an attachment to a particular teacher, may well need to reject you before you 'reject' them (by leaving, or by letting them go to another class or similar) - hence the bad behaviour. Many of these children and young people will have experienced sudden loss or upheaval with no processing of the feelings, no-one to help them make sense of what they are feeling or thinking. They may have been left with overwhelming anxiety and upset, and will do anything to avoid feeling this again. We should remember that anxious children do not always look anxious. Anxiety can show in clowning around, fighting and being aggressive or even in physical illnesses.

Many teachers are advised not to let pupils know that they are leaving until the last possible moment. The concern is that the pupils will stop accepting the teacher's authority and 'play up' for the remaining weeks of term. However, the impact of a sudden departure can be upsetting for everyone, especially pupils who have had other previous experience of sudden and painful endings. It is far better to plan the ending, giving plenty of advance warning and allowing all of you, the pupils and the teacher, to acknowledge the feelings brought up by needing to say goodbye.

Robert's farwell 'French Week'

Robert is an NQT and French teacher in a large secondary school considered challenging to teach in. At the beginning of the year he took over some classes who had only ever had supply teachers or teachers who did not stay long. After some initial struggles and battles to win their trust and respect, his last term with them has been productive; he finally feels he is getting somewhere with the students.

Unfortunately, due to family circumstances, Robert will have to move schools next year and he wants to provide a good ending for his classes. Other teachers in the staffroom have told him to make sure no-one knows he is leaving until the last week of term - otherwise he 'will be in for trouble'. Robert feels uncomfortable with this idea and decides to plan the ending so that it can be a celebration of the work done and an acknowledgement of his own sadness at moving on. He decides to have a 'French Week', where his classes prepare food, invite visitors in, show their work and give short presentations on France. His classes spend a lot of time and effort on preparing this, and surprise him with cards written in French, wishing him well and saying they will miss him.

In this example, Robert manages to mark the ending of his relationship with his pupils by celebrating their joint achievements. They are able to respond by acknowledging their sadness at his departure. He has allowed them to fully experience the feelings involved in a transition and to realise that this is an important and necessary part of life.

Implications for the teacher

The transitions and endings which form a normal part of school life give us an opportunity as teachers to show these children another model of endings. They can learn that it is acceptable and normal to have a myriad of powerful and sometimes conflicting feelings. They might feel angry at the teacher and like and miss them at the same time. We can show them by our actions and words that these feelings can be thought about, contained and tolerated, that they do not have to suppress them, ignore them or hide away with them.

We can help them to understand that someone can go away and still 'hold you in mind', and how this doesn't diminish or destroy the relationship. They can learn that you, the teacher, and they, the pupils, can hold onto the memories of what they have learned. They can thus begin to be less apprehensive about change and even start to look forward to the positives of moving on.

Teaching Strategies

If we begin to see transitions in this way, we can easily develop some ideas for marking the ritual and learning from it. Some ideas I have found useful are:

- ✔ If possible, work up until the last minute of term. These children cannot bear the uncertainty of lack of structure. If this is not possible, have some mechanical structured activities for them to do even if they are off timetable
- ✔ Let children know in advance if someone is leaving and arrange a proper opportunity to mark the occasion. Marking goodbyes honours and

respects the relationship developed

- ✔ Have a leaving party
- ✔ Mark the changing of relationships with other pupils as well. One idea might be to write everybody's names on paper and pass the slips around for the pupils to write something they like about that person, or will remember about them
- ✔ Have a final Circle Time to allow people to say what they are feeling
- ✔ Create a group photo or picture
- ✔ Get children to write letters to themselves or to new children. Write a letter yourself to the class and let them read it privately
- ✔ Make a memory book - your best moments in this class
- ✔ Encourage a review of work, what we were like and what we have learnt
- ✔ Make use of stories, journeys are good ones to read or make up. A child can write a collaborative story about a journey which involves the idea of moving on
- ✔ Make use of appropriate symbolic activities - tidying up, putting away, sorting things out
- ✔ Don't take things down off the walls whilst the children are still around

All these activities are examples of marking an ending in the 'proper' way.
(For more ideas about transitions and ending, see Bomber, *2007)*

Dealing with our own feelings about endings

We need to be sure that we are not projecting our own feelings about endings onto the children and young people we are working with. In my experience, it can be difficult for key staff to let go of children with whom they have had a close working relationship, and for whom they still have anxiety about the future.

Sheila's anxiety about leaving her students

Sheila was a teacher who was concerned about leaving her job. She worked closely with a group of vulnerable young people whose behaviour had been of great concern in the school. She had established good relationships with them, and there had been a noticeable improvement in their behaviour. She was worried that they would not be able to cope with the loss of the key attachment figure she felt she had become for them.

She had been covering for a year on maternity leave. The young people knew this and they knew that she had been looking for a full-time position. Nevertheless, she was very anxious about the actual ending, particularly as it got pushed forward when she got a new job with an earlier start date.

She decided to tell the young people individually and then do a group ending. One boy said "Don't worry about it Miss, you have to earn money and have a life, we know that, thanks for your help this year."

She realised that a lot of the issues around ending had been hers and that done properly, these young people could cope with her moving on. There were tears and sadness at her leaving meeting, but it was an appropriate reaction, and she felt it had been a positive experience for everyone, including herself.

Allowing the acknowledgement of these sad feelings, as well as the anticipation of moving on showed the young people that a transition can be frightening, sad and exciting at the same time. As Barrett & Trevitt (1991) put it:

> Thinking about some of the difficulties as well as the pleasures of moving on can remind the individual that painful experiences can be thought about. (p. 116)

In summary

Beginnings, transitions and endings can be very difficult times for children and young people who have experienced disruption and trauma. Such changes can evoke and remind them of losses and other often sudden, traumatic and unsatisfactory endings. There are things which class teachers can do to help them manage these situations.

- Plan an ending in advance wherever possible. Be clear about dates and plan a proper event to mark the ending. Avoid the temptation to postpone telling them until the last minute. If you have had good classroom management, it will not disappear overnight

- Allow time for children to mark their sadness at the ending and honour the relationships. They may express this as anger or rejection, but bear in mind this is a normal part of the loss process.

- Acknowledge your own feelings to them. If it is hard to leave, let them know. Do not be afraid of marking endings and be aware that some of the feelings you are attributing to the group may indeed be your own

- Have a tangible product for them and you to take away, such as a group photo or memory book

- Spend some time looking at the positives of transitions and changes
- If possible, liaise with new staff and arrange for pupils to meet their new teacher or find out information about the new school situation
- If your class is moving on, get them to write letters to your next class about what to expect and what it is like in your class, so that they can acknowledge their own learning and development

Chapter 10

Developing our skills in reaching these 'unteachables'

In the previous chapters I have shown how an understanding of some key therapeutic theories can shed light on what may be happening with these 'unteachable ' children, and what they 'do' to us, the adults who work with them. As a classroom teacher, these ideas have certainly helped me in managing my own feelings around my work, and have decreased some of the anxiety and frustration I felt at seemingly not being able to help these pupils.

However, like most teachers, I also wanted there to be concrete things I could work on, skills I could practise, to learn to deal better with these unteachable children and young people in the longer-term. Such skill development might still not mean that I could prevent crises arising; but might put me in a better position to manage my relationships with pupils so that I could deal with these inevitable setbacks in a more resourceful way. In this section, I will set out some of the techniques I, and the staff I have worked with, have found most useful to develop in our day-to-day teaching.

KEY SKILL 1 NOTICING THINGS IN A DIFFERENT WAY

The ability to observe these children from new perspectives, to notice what is happening between us in school and in the classroom, is a fundamental skill worth practising. As a therapist, I became used to taking and using time to reflect on the child's behaviour and words, and what these might mean. This skill can be used in the following ways by a classroom teacher:

✓ Stepping back and thinking about the meaning of a behaviour

When faced with challenging behaviour, we need to stop and think what the behaviour is communicating. It can be helpful to re-frame the question, and ask ourselves -

- What is the *underlying need* that this behaviour is trying to communicate?
- What does the child need, and therefore need to have or learn from us? What have they not had sufficient experience of, in order to behave appropriately?

✓ Reflecting about the meaning of their behaviour using ideas from therapeutic thinking

Using ideas explained in previous chapters, you could choose to

- Think about the child's stage of emotional development rather than their chronological age (Chapter 3)
- Think about the unconscious defence mechanisms you might be observing. Could there be projection, displacement or transference in operation? (Chapter 6)
- Notice when blaming and splitting occur so that you can strive to avoid them (Chapter 6).
- Notice the pupil's pattern of relating. Where is he engaged? What kind of words does she use again and again? In particular, pay attention to any underlying attachment patterns - ambivalent/resistant, avoidant or disorganised? What classroom strategies would address these attachment needs? (Chapter 7)
- Observe what stage of play the pupil has reached and whether it is appropriate for learning (Chapter 8)
- Notice if his or her behaviour is affected by beginnings, endings and/or transitions. Plan accordingly (Chapter 9)

Observing and noticing our pupils' behaviour like this can lead to the key skill of re-framing.

KEY SKILL 2 RE-FRAMING

This is a fundamental strategy for dealing with these children. Re-framing their behaviour means looking for alternative explanations that see a behaviour as an attempt to communicate with us, telling us something about the child's need or state of mind. We can never really know the true meaning of someone else's behaviour, even if we know the person well: we are essentially mind-reading when we ascribe meaning to a behaviour. It follows, therefore, that we can choose how we view a specific behaviour and this will affect how we react to it. For example, a young person who continually truants lessons could be seen as running away from himself or learning, and not just avoiding work.

> *I was working in a school where the fire alarm was continually set off by the same small group of boys. The Head was incensed, and could not understand why they insisted on being so 'stupid' - particularly as they always got caught and punished. Another teacher commented that they were all boys who were not succeeding in school, with very chaotic backgrounds, and "Wasn't it interesting that the fire alarm was like a loud cry for help?". The Head was amazed and thanked the teacher for giving her another way of seeing this behaviour. The thought eventually led to case reviews and small group work with these children around their learning and emotional needs.*

KEY SKILL 3 BREAKING THE EXPECTED PATTERN OF RESPONSE

As I explained previously, many of these children are experts at drawing us into the pattern of behaviour which they are used to. Practise recognising these patterns. The behaviour is usually something which will have happened in your way of relating with them more than twice, that feels outside your normal range of behaviour. Notice what you are being pulled into, and try to do something different.

Ms Christie does something different

Eddie was a fourteen year old boy who seemed to be an expert in 'winding teachers up'. He managed to provoke the most mild-mannered teachers into raising their voices and sending him out of their lessons. His Science teacher, Ms Christie, decided that she wanted to try to change this pattern of relating. The next time she found herself getting annoyed with Eddie she consciously took a deep breath, a long step back and said, "I can feel myself getting annoyed and I find that interesting. It's interesting that this seems to be our normal pattern and I'm wondering how that happens. What do we both get out of it?" Eddie looked shocked, then laughed sheepishly and said, "Dunno, just seems normal to me". Ms Christie was able to reply that sometimes things which seem normal might not be the best way to do things. She suggested that they both try to find a different way to talk to each other. Eddie did not immediately respond but the next time Ms Christie started to get annoyed, she was able to comment again on how interesting it was and to wonder if it had just become a habit which was hard to break. Eventually, she realised that she was not getting so angry so often with Eddie and he seemed to settle more in her lessons. She had managed to break the pattern.

What Ms Christie did in the above example was not so important. What was important was that she *did something different.*

KEY SKILL 4 USING LANGUAGE DIFFERENTLY

Our use of language affects much of what happens in our classes. We can probably all remember comments made to us by teachers - positive and negative - which stayed with us into adulthood. By paying attention to and monitoring your own use of language, you can give students an experience of being thought about by a caring adult. You can practise and extend your use of language in the following ways:

✔ Being specific about social and emotional skills

Notice and acknowledge appropriate use of social and emotional skills such as empathy. Name these skills specifically. In particular, notice if students are demonstrating the skills we know help promote learning in a class, such as self-awareness and self-management, empathy and awareness of others, good listening, good waiting to be helped, and turn-taking.

This is very often done well by primary teachers, who may be used to focusing on child development, but can be neglected at secondary level as we often assume that students have these skills by the age of eleven.

✔ Wondering aloud and providing commentaries which describe what might be happening on an emotional level

This is a very powerful technique and one which we can borrow very naturally from the world of therapy. As teachers, we are used to commenting on behaviour, but not on the possible underlying reasons for or feelings behind the behaviour. *Wondering aloud* is a technique which allows us to explore reasons with the students in a non-directive way. It is similar to the technique of 'reverie' which Bion (1970) observed in mothers trying to name the overwhelming feelings an infant might be having.

For example:

"I can see you are really angry. I'm wondering if it is because you feel no-one is listening to you".

"I wonder if it is all getting a bit too confusing now"
"I'm wondering if everyone is feeling a bit stuck. That can feel very frustrating and sometimes makes us feel like giving up".

Commentary is a similar technique which can bring in a more logical left brain way of thinking in times of stress. The adult makes concrete comments about what is happening for the child, either internally or externally or both. Commentaries can be factual or related to what the child might be feeling. They may not be completely accurate but they can help a child make sense of their experience. They are most effective when the adult has already built up a trusting relationship with the child. For example, you might say:

"OK, I can see you are getting fidgety now, you are looking out of the window, tapping your pencil and sighing. Maybe you are finding it difficult to concentrate and need to do something to get your brain focused again. How about taking a deep breath and remembering there are only ten minutes to go?"

Or the commentary can be related to a potential internal anxiety:

"You are looking a bit fed up now. Losing in a game can be difficult to accept and maybe you feel like giving up and it's ok to feel like that. Everyone loses sometimes. That's part of the fun in the game. Let's play it again and see what happens."

(*See* Bomber 2007 pp. 95-98 *for more information on using commentaries*)

✔ Using commentaries with the whole class

Be prepared to name what is going on to the rest of the class.

"We know that John is working on waiting for attention, so think about how we can all help with this."

One way to do this is to generalise about a problem someone might be having and not make it specific to an individual. For example:

> *"It's sometimes difficult to stop calling out and wait patiently. Has anyone got any ideas how to remember to do this?"*

✔ Containing overwhelming emotion rather than jumping to reassure and solve

It is very tempting and only natural to want to reassure a distressed child or young person that everything will be alright. However, sometimes when we do this we are not acknowledging the depth and validity of their emotion. We are in danger of dismissing it if we say *"Don't be upset, there's nothing to worry about really"*. We can stay with the emotion and help the pupil process it by saying something like: "*Yes, that is really upsetting, and it would be normal to feel really bad about it.*"

✔ Really listening - to the feeling as well as the words

Think about the last conversation you had with a child or young person who is difficult to teach. Did you listen to the end of their sentences, or were you already thinking about your response? Did you listen and reflect back a feeling, or were you anxious to provide a suggestion and solution? Did you listen as if you had time or were you aware of a time pressure, to get on to the next thing in your busy day? We like to think we are good listeners. But generally we tend to listen through our own filters. Sometimes we listen to the first part of a sentance and then half way through, start thinking how to reply. When dealing with a disruptive student, we often don't hear their story, as we have our own goal - to get them back on track as soon as possible. Make a conscious effort to practise active listening and allow pauses for thinking. Reflect back to the student the feeling coming through the conversation. Small as this seems, it can make a big difference in a busy school.

KEY SKILL 5 THE ABILITY TO UNDERSTAND AND REFLECT ON THE REAL PROCESS OF CHANGE

It is very difficult to change a behaviour or habit that we have had for many years. It may have served us well. Simply wanting to change is not enough. Often in schools we think that a student who has agreed to a target is deliberately not keeping to it. But life is rarely so simple.

It can be useful to remember something about the process of making lasting change. Use the model of the Motivational Cycle (*described in* Chapter 3) to remember that relapses are important learning events. These are the times when we learn what we need to do differently in order to make the changes we want. A relapse is so often the stage when we give up with these troubled children, saying *"They have had so much help and still can't get it right"*. Remember that just being in a safe environment now or for a short time will not automatically mean everything is alright. Behaviour will not immediately transform by itself - it takes time, feedback about what is and is not working, and usually the support and encouragement of others.

KEY SKILL 6 PLANNING

As teachers, we are used to spending time planning lessons according to the syllabus and the abilities of our students. We need to develop our ability to create tasks and plan lessons from a different starting point. We can learn to build in tasks which are based on what we have noticed might be happening unconsciously. Sometimes a slight shift in emphasis can make all the difference. When planning your lessons and tasks:

✔ Consider the child's emotional developmental level

You may be teaching a group of fourteen year olds, but some may have the developmental level of a five year old in terms of social and emotional skills. It may be necessary to plan a task which promotes the skills you want them to learn. Give feedback on this aspect of the task - how well they listened and worked together - as well as on the task itself.

Take every opportunity in the curriculum to name skills such as empathy and make them explicit. For example, in a history or geography lesson, you might ask the pupils to imagine what it was like to live in a different time or culture. When they offer good insights into this, you can say *"Well done, you showed very good empathy in your answers because you were really able to imagine what it was like to be someone else."*

✔ Plan for the potential need to calm down agitated, anxious or hyper-vigilant children

This is differentiation but with a therapeutic reason. We know that mechanical, repetitive tasks such as sorting, putting things together, putting things in boxes and so on can make the left brain kick in and calm down an agitated child. Part of our planning may need to include having this type of activity to hand if required.

✔ Include games in the lesson plan

Some games can teach a specific play skill and allow emotions to be expressed in a contained way. They involve a two-way level playing field which engages the child who needs to be omnipotent or who cannot bear to be taught. Games can be developed which create opportunities to practice new skills in safe ways. Skills that need to be practised by these children will include: asking for help, relaxing, resolving conflict, for example with scripts, having fun without getting out-of-control. Some of my favourite games are:

• I'LL ANSWER FOR YOU

Students work in groups of four. One student sits on a chair and two students stand behind. The fourth student asks questions to the student on the chair. Questions should be about the student - their likes/ dislikes and so on. The student on the chair remains silent and the two standing behind have to answer the questions for him. They have to try to imagine what his answers would be. The student on the chair simply nods or shakes his head to indicate how accurate the answer is. The students take turns in the different positions. This game is an excellent practice of the skill of empathy, 'walking in someone else's shoes'. It can also show students how they come across to others.

The content of the questions can be changed to reflect topics being taught but the basic skill of empathy is the main focus.

• MIMING

Students work in small groups. One student from each group is given a sentence or piece of information to mime.

The others have to guess what it is and send someone back to the teacher to tell them. This can also be developed as an activity where students mime conversation to each other. Any activity like this is an excellent way to practise the skill of building rapport and paying close attention to someone else's way of communicating.

• BACKS TO THE BOARD

Students work in small groups. They take it in turns to come to the board. One student from the first group sits with their back to the board, and the other four or five students sit in a line facing the board. The teacher writes a key word, definition or piece of information on the board. The other students have to get the student with their back to the board to say the exact word(s). They can say anything except for any part of the word or information. When they get it, they all change around and another student has their back to the board. The aim is to see how many items can be got right in a time-limit, such as two minutes. Then another group comes to the board. This game develops a lot of skills - listening, explaining so that someone else can understand, working as a group and learning to work together in a fun way. Again, these are skills many of these 'unteachable' children have never learned.

Be careful, though, as children and young people will need to learn to PLAY these games! If you stop the game and refuse to play it until they can play it properly, they will never learn. If there are problems, stop the game and help the group reflect on what was going wrong and what needs to happen for it to work well the next time. Remember we learn through our mistakes!

Circle Time in an excellent way of developing these skills and can be used very successfully in secondary schools if it is linked to learning to learn skills. *(For more on Circle Time games, see Mosley 1996)*

KEY SKILL 7 WORKING WITH METAPHOR

Planning in creative work which revolves around a theme or metaphor can be very helpful for helping children reveal, explore and perhaps resolve conflicts, anxieties and developmental blocks. Every subject can incorporate an element of this, not only the obvious choices of English and Drama. The use of DVDs and books which show people in real or fictional situations can be used to discuss how certain characters felt and what led to their actions. Students can be asked to draw representations based on their reactions to materials. One useful task is to encourage them to draw in frames (like a cartoon strip). In some strange way this seems to help contain any emotion or anxiety in the activity. Keeping work in boxes can also signify containment.

KEY SKILL 8 WORKING ON AND MANAGING YOURSELF

No-one is perfect. Students with challenging behaviour often recognise when things have gone too far and appreciate a teacher's honesty in trying to address the situation. This is not about 'saving face' or apportioning blame, it is about modelling adult behaviour.

✔ Recognising what is 'ours' and what is 'theirs'

Be prepared to reflect on the reasons for an incident or class not going well. How much really came from you, and how much was from them?

Ms Holden loses her sense of humour

I was working with Ms Holden who continually had rows with a certain very challenging pupil. To find Kathy challenging was not unusual within the staff team, but it was unusual for this particular teacher, as she often had great success with this type of pupil.

When Ms Holden had calmed down, she acknowledged that some of her anger was at herself for not being able to deal with the child's jokes, when she prided herself on having a great sense of humour! Also, she felt very unsupported by her Head of Department, and this had started to play on her mind as exams were approaching. This was resulting in her having much less patience with this student than previously.

Once she had acknowledged these things to herself, she was able to think about using her usual successful strategies with Kathy. They still had their 'blow-ups', but she felt better able to manage the situation and repair it afterwards.

✔ Be your own best friend

If you find yourself despairing and thinking you must be hopeless because you cannot teach a certain child, take a moment and think about what advice you would give your best friend in this situation. You probably would not berate and de-motivate them by saying they should give up teaching! And yet, we often have an internal voice which does just that to us. Take the advice you would give someone else. It will usually put you in a better frame of mind.

✔ Things we can change and things we cannot change

We usually spend a lot of time worrying about things over which we actually have no control. We cannot predict that a colleague will be stuck in traffic and we will have to cover. We cannot predict that a child's grandparent will die suddenly.

> PAUSE FOR THOUGHT
>
> **Look back at the two lists you made in Chapter 4, (things you were worried about p.56)**
>
> Decide what you want to happen for an item on the 'can control' list, and take the first step towards doing it
>
> Put those items where you don't have any control into a separate compartment in your mind, and give yourself permission to think about them at another more appropriate time

✔ Six highlights of each day

As teachers we tend to dwell on those students we could not teach, those classes which did not go well, those parents who complained. This can be emotionally unhealthy, negatively affecting our state of well-being and de-motivating us.

At the end of each day, write down your six highlights. This could include things that went well, pupils who learned, pupils who behaved, laughs you had in the staffroom, anything can be used. It might seem forced and strange at first. Our brains might not be used to such positive thinking, but by asking ourselves "*What is working well?*", we will cope better with the stressful situations. We will be in a resourceful state for thinking about the stressful situations and remember why we want to be teachers! Steps with these children will usually be small but we need to pay attention to that progress.

✔ Allowing ourselves not to be perfect

This might seem a strange comment, but in my experience of working with teachers across the world, there is one driving force - the desire to get it 'right'. This is, of course, a commendable desire. However, when dealing with people and relationships, especially those children who are the topic of this book, there is no hundred percent formula, no way to get it 'right' all the time, because, quite simply we are all only human.

In his description of how infants develop emotional security, Winnicott talks about 'good-enough' mothering (1971). This refers to the fact that an infant needs his mother to be attuned to his needs and able to think about them. But he does not need a 'perfect' mother who can predict and understand every little response. Trying to be perfect can have the opposite effect, because if we try to do everything for these children, we can either become too controlling or get too frustrated when we cannot find an instant 'solution'. Part of learning is learning to bear the frustration of not knowing, of learning through feedback on mistakes. We need to remember this for ourselves.

Relief

I was training a group of teachers who work in a unit for excluded pupils. After I had explained the theories of psychological defence mechanisms, the newest teacher in the team sighed and said, "Thank God. I thought I felt like this because I am only new and not confident or good enough in what I am doing."

Almost immediately the Head of Centre said, "Well, I'm relieved, because I have days when I feel really useless and then I think I should know better because I have been teaching for years!"

KEY SKILL 9 THE ABILITY TO WORK WELL WITH AND SEEK SUPPORT FROM OTHER AGENCIES

Setting up support networks which can contain all the different feelings these children and young people provoke in the adults working with them is vital. This is not a new idea but, as I have explained earlier, it can be difficult to avoid splitting of opinions and feelings. We need to ensure we have multi-agency meetings which are not set up to create a blame/justification culture between agencies. Acknowledging our own difficulties and feelings at the beginning of any such meeting can be a good way to start. If you are involved in such meetings, spend some time getting to know how the systems of different agencies operate. Apply to go on some joint training. Don't be afraid to admit not knowing something and ringing up for some advice and alternative suggestions from another agency. If possible, set up regular meetings around these children, so that there are structured spaces for thinking together rather than instant gatherings called reactively and probably at very short notice in an emergency.

KEY SKILL 10 DEALING WITH PARENTS/CARERS

We all know that dealing with parents/carers can be a key part of our work as teachers, and yet there is little preparation for it in training. As I said at the beginning of this book, these children bring up all sorts of feelings in the adults around them, feelings of failure, blame, hopelessness, anger, despair. If we are not careful, these overwhelming feelings take over and cause splitting around the child, leading us to feel annoyed and blaming towards the parents. It is essential that we honour and respect the parents in our work with them, even if we feel they have some responsibility for their children's behaviour in school. Going in with an attitude of blame will not lead to a productive meeting or ability to work together for the child's best interests.

We need to acknowledge the child's strengths, thank the parents for coming up and being interested, focus on what is working and empathise with the difficulties in dealing with some of these children. We need to use inclusive language - *"What can we do together about this?"* - and keep in close contact, feeding back positive as well as negative experiences.

The blame game

I was working with a girl in school who had been excluded several times for abusive language and aggressive behaviour towards staff. The Headteacher had told me that she had called the mother and the mother had put the phone down on her. The mother told me that the Headteacher had said her children were scum, that she was not a good parent and that she was not wasting any more money on a psychotherapist for the girl.

I felt myself in danger of getting angry with one or the other or both of them. When talking to the Head I was annoyed at the mother for not listening, and when talking to the mother, I was annoyed at the Head for not perservering.

Of course, I did not know the truth about what had been said, but both the Headteacher and the parent had described the exchange from their very real perspective of what had happened. I needed to try to empathise with the strong feelings of not knowing what to do and try to get the two of them to focus on the shared things we all had in common - frustration at what was not working, and the search for what might work for a positive future outcome for the child.

I have to say that I was not successful in this case: the situation had become very entrenched, and I did not know enough about the school dynamics to turn this around. I believe I would have had a greater chance of success if I had been a member of the teaching staff who could work in the overall context.

PUTTING ALL THE SKILLS TOGETHER

"But won't all this take too long?" This is the objection often raised when I introduce teachers to these different perspectives and ways of working. In my experience, it doesn't take a specific block of time, which we would need to carve out from our already tightly-packed schedules. What it requires is a slight shift in thinking and focus. We can test out this objection, with the simple reflection task below. How long does applying a different way of thinking really take?

Paul - a 'demonised' child

Paul was in year 10. He was considered to be bright and capable of achieving high GCSE grades. However, he spent much of his time in the Head of Year's office or on temporary exclusions because of his aggressive behaviour, fighting and arguing with teachers.

Several teachers thought he should be permanently excluded. They said he had no interest in anyone else except himself and he was a danger to others. He had recently been excluded from the technology workshops for health and safety reasons. In the last few weeks he had told the Head of Technology to "Shut up, you silly dwarf": picked up a year 8 boy and held him upside down until he cried: been sent off in a key football match for arguing with the referee: told the History teacher that he needed anger management and he could take him on any time if he wanted: and not attended for the past three days, because he said he had been sent home and told not to come back, even though his Head of Year said Paul had not been excluded.

PAUSE FOR THOUGHT

What is your immediate reaction to this account of Paul and his behaviour?

What extra information would you like to know?

What underlying defence mechanisms might be in operation?

What might be the attachment pattern?

What needs might this boy be trying to fulfill ?

How could this boy's actions be re-framed with a positive intention?

What needs to happen to maintain a focus on learning and teaching?

Some extra information

Some of the key adults involved with Paul in this school knew that he came from an abusive, alcoholic background. His father had been shot when he was seven, and there had been a lot of negative publicity about him and a potential criminal connection. There had been rumours that his mother had paid for the 'hit'. After his father's death, his mother had begun drinking heavily, and was often not at home in the evenings.

In primary school, Paul had said that he found reading difficult and that his dad had spent a lot of time helping him improve.

PAUSE FOR THOUGHT

What do you think now?

What pattern would Paul be used to creating and provoking ?

What emotional and mental state would it be important to maintain as his teacher?

What are you now thinking about his anxieties, defences and attachment patterns?

I would say that Paul was exhibiting omnipotence as a defence, that his attachment pattern was fairly avoidant, and that he was keen to reject adults before they rejected him. On the other hand, he could focus very effectively on an independent learning task but wanted staff to be available for him when he wanted.

He also provoked most staff into getting angry and rejecting him, something which I felt was familiar to him. Although this boy looked and acted in many ways older than his years, having had to take care of himself from an early age, in some ways he was a much younger child, not yet able to play by others' rules and unable to ask for help for fear of humiliation.

There was also a lot of splitting around Paul. Staff were either very 'for' or 'against' keeping him in school, and he was the subject of endless discussions in the staffroom. He needed staff to be able to think about him in a containing way and for them to be consistent in how they addressed his needs. We needed to encourage his desire for independent learning, not reject it, and show him we could be available to help, for example, in after-school revision clubs.

In summary

We can work to develop skills which will help us understand and relate to these 'unteachable' children and young people. These skills involve learning to step back and think about what is happening in a different way. Eventually they may lead us to develop additional teaching strategies.

Chapter 11

How can we develop a whole school approach to underpin this work?

In my workshops, teachers sometimes say "*That's all well and good, but the Head would never let us do these things in my school*". It is true that we are affected by the environment in which we operate. If we feel that we are being scrutinised and blamed for every little mistake, we will inevitably find it hard to be thoughtful about these children and their problems. If we work in an emotionally literate climate, we will feel more able to admit to our mistakes, be honest about our feelings and communicate more openly with others. However, that does not mean we can ONLY do this if our senior leadership agrees with us. There are still things we can do as individual teachers.

In this section, therefore, I will look at how whole school culture might be affected by the ideas in the previous chapters. I will begin by looking at what can be done if you have some influence at leadership level in your school, and the benefits of incorporating these ideas throughout the school system. I will then look at how you might still influence the system by your own actions, or maintain your positive state, if you feel your new approach will challenge the ethos of your school culture.

It is not always immediately obvious if a school is a 'container' for feelings and allows real thinking to take place, or not. What is going on underneath the surface can be very different from what appears to be happening on the outside.

Look at the two case studies which follow on pp.174-5, and consider which school seems to be thinking most reflectively, and which is developing the most emotionally literate climate.

School X

School X is a large comprehensive school. It has been consistently underperforming and parents are reluctant to send their children there due to bad publicity. It is seen as the 'last choice'. On the surface, the teachers seem to be coping, are always pleasant to each other and often socialising together. In the staffroom they laugh and joke with each other and engage in 'banter', with certain teachers often being the butt of the jokes. These teachers seem happy to accept the teasing.

The staff rarely speak about the children in their classes, saying they need to 'switch off' in their breaks. They speak even more rarely about their own teaching. They sympathise with the children's situation, saying that they understand some of the pupils have very difficult home lives which interfere with their education. They accept that some of these children cannot attain high levels.

They do not believe there is much point in telephoning some parents, as "*they are not interested and never come in*". There is a small, committed group of parents who attend meetings and run the PTA but generally, parents do not visit the school.

Staff attend one meeting a week, either departmental or pastoral and sometimes have a whole school meeting. The atmosphere at these meetings is friendly and humorous. For example, just before Christmas there is always much hilarity at the staff meeting where presents from 'Secret Santa' are opened.

The Learning Support staff have their own corner of the staffroom and their own workbase. Children who have special needs, particularly behaviour, are dealt with by a specialist unit. All staff praise the staff in this unit highly but very few of them ever work over there or provide work for the children who are in the unit.

School Y

School Y is a smaller school in a similar area. It is also underperforming although results have improved in the last year. The staffroom is a lively place, with staff often coming in and ranting about their last class or a particular student. Colleagues appear supportive but will also suggest strategies or offer to help.

There are often impromptu after-school or lunchtime meetings, where staff meet to discuss a particular student and share strategies. Some classes are on behaviour programmes, where all staff teaching them have agreed to monitor progress in a class behaviour book. Staff volunteer to mentor certain pupils throughout the school who have behavioural difficulties.

The staff empathise with their pupils, knowing that many have very difficult home circumstances, but they do not believe this stops them getting on in school.

Staff want to find a way to work with the pupil, parent and school. Parents often come in angry, shouting at staff about incidents or requests to come in, but usually they can be calmed down enough to discuss the situation. The school has been trying to set up parent support groups and is now considering holding them in a local café to see if more parents would attend.

There is a specialist unit and some staff work over there or drop in to see pupils in their non-teaching time. The staff and head of the unit sometimes have heated discussions about certain pupils and how to deal with them.

The staff do not socialise much together but end-of-term events are well-attended. Most staff attend at least two meetings a week - departmental and often cross-curricular, although the second meeting is not compulsory.

The Learning Support Staff have recently, under duress, been moved out of their own special room and into the staffroom where they now sit with other staff at lunchtime. Some staff eat their lunch with pupils. There is a weekly staff support group which meets to discuss leadership and issues that are making the job difficult at the moment. This is facilitated by an outside consultant.

WHO IS TAKING CARE OF EMOTIONAL NEEDS?

Which school has the highest morale? In which school are the emotional needs of the staff being taken care of? It might seem that this is happening in school X, as the staff are friendly and socialise together. However, they do not appear to attend to what Bion calls the 'primary task' (1961, 1970) - which in a school, would be teaching and learning and creating thinking around the children. They have low expectations of the children and maybe of themselves for working in such a school.

In school Y, the emotional climate is more vibrant. Staff are more prepared to challenge each other in a safe way. They are able to think about the needs of the students, since their own needs for safety and belonging are also being met. Staff are prepared to spend extra time on meetings and discussions, as they feel it helps their teaching and it also helps the children. They all have a sense of responsibility for those children with additional needs. In school X, the children with additional needs are actually seen as a special group to be taken away and have something 'magical' done to them, in order to return to mainstream.

HOW DOES A SCHOOL CREATE A SUPPORTIVE EMOTIONAL CLIMATE?

The emotionally open and honest climate in school Y has not happened by accident. There has been work done at a whole-school leadership level to facilitate this and individual teachers have also worked to support it. I will now look at what can help - both at senior leadership and classroom teacher level - to create schools in which staff and pupils can take time to think about feelings and reflect on the meaning of seemingly inexplicable behaviour.

✔ There is a commitment from senior leadership

It is easier to think about the children and young people we find 'unteachable', and take appropriate time to reflect, if there is a commitment from senior managers to this way of thinking. Concepts such as the development of emotional literacy need to be on the agenda of whole school improvement plans, and this requires direction from the senior leadership team. Initiatives such as SEAL are bringing these ideas into schools but they need to be seen in the context of schools spending time on the 'processing' of teachers' feelings, as well as those of the pupils (in other words, building in time for teachers to think about their own emotional reponses to certain situations and pupils, and how these affect their teaching). Taking time to reflect on what might be happening to us as teachers and in the relationships in the classroom is not easy. There will always be other priorities if the link is not made between these issues and learning. Some senior managers and teachers might see this as 'pink and fluffy stuff', and not part of the real job of teaching. However, it is a vital component in moving a school on in the way described above.

A school was introducing the concept of how teachers' feelings might be affected by pupil behaviour. One member of staff reacted angrily, and said that she was sick of discussions like this, where the emphasis was always on why staff had to change and adapt. She said that it should not always be the staff who were seen to be at fault, and that the pupils had to change as well. She felt that she had a right to be angry when certain pupils were rude, disrespectful and would not behave in her classes.

The facilitator said she was right, it was legitimate to feel angry and frustrated about that. It was not the feelings themselves that were at issue, but how we managed them.

The group realised that they had done this kind of work with pupils but not with their own staff. This teacher was very often angry and argumentative and it seemed her overwhelming feelings were getting in the way of her teaching. Being allowed to express those feelings and have them validated was an important step for her.

✔ Sharing failures as well as successes

Staff - particularly senior staff - need to be prepared to talk about their feelings and share their experience of failure as well as their success. When we do staff training, we tend to focus on what works and sometimes present things as if there is a perfect way to deal with challenges. With experience, we know there is often a trial-and-error approach to real life. Senior managers need to make sure they are making this clear to people. For example, it might be helpful for staff to hear you share your feelings about what it was like to move into management.

A teacher who had recently been promoted was upset because members of staff seemed to be very critical of any ideas she was putting forward in Continuing Professional Development (CPD). A member of the Senior Leadership Team (SLT) took her aside and said that she had also felt like this when she first joined SLT. She had felt that she was no longer part of the 'staff-room' gang and had to re-think her socialising in terms of her peer group. She said she had found the step up quite lonely, and that it became very important to pursue other friendships outside the staff group.

The younger member of staff felt relieved to hear that she was not the only one going through this, and to have confirmation that managing relationships is a key part of leadership.

WHAT THE INDIVIDUAL TEACHER CAN DO - IF SENIOR STAFF DO NOT DISCLOSE THEIR FEELINGS

In most schools, senior staff do not walk around telling everyone how they feel! In fact, they often don't have time for this type of discussion. However, that does not mean they will be unwilling to respond if asked at an appropriate moment. You can ask a well-timed question in your line-management meetings, or you can perhaps have a more informal chat on a training day or after-school event. Being honest about your own feelings in your new position and asking them if they ever felt like that, can elicit some surprising answers. If you feel there is no-one on senior management you could approach, try finding like-minded staff in a similar position (*see below for ideas*) or reading books on leadership in business which often cover these topics.

✔ Creating space in the time-table for staff to think about their work with the child

I have shown in previous chapters how important it is to make time for staff to think about and reflect on the needs and behaviour of these seemingly unteachable pupils. This can work well if it can be timetabled into the school day. The following example shows how one school did this.

> *A school was having problems with various students and several people seemed to be involved. The staff had tried to meet after school and in lunch-breaks to come up with a plan and exchange ideas, but it was all very rushed and reactive 'firefighting'. They took the matter to the Pastoral Head, who arranged with SLT for these key people to have a fortnightly time-tabled meeting, with cover, to discuss certain cases.*
>
> *This eventually led to much better thinking and solutions. The meetings began with each member naming a pupil they were concerned about and the group discussing what they knew and what they thought might be going on for the pupil. Although at first there was resistance to the idea of a timetabled meeting, as cover had to be arranged in some cases, it quickly became apparent that the plans being made at these meetings were more effective and helped everyone in their dealing with the children.*

Comment from the Pastoral Head:

"I did not really think having meetings was a good idea when one of my Heads of Year suggested it. I just thought they had no idea about the difficulties of timetabling and cover for colleagues to attend meetings. However, the Head of Year who suggested it was adamant that it would save us time in the long-term and make everyone's lives easier when dealing with these pupils. So I decided we should give it a go for one term. I am amazed at how much better we are at dealing with pupils and how much easier it is to recognise where the real issues are."

✔ What can the individual teacher do?

If your school will not timetable these meetings or you are not part of them, it is, of course, possible to make time to have these discussions with colleagues in your department and others who support your ideas. It will be time well spent. You can also be pro-active in trying to persuade key people to think about timetabling meeting time for planning. The argument against it is usually that there is not time in the school day for staff to be taken away from teaching. In my experience, far more time is wasted if these pro-active meetings do not take place. After all, how many hours are spent on disciplining pupils, phoning parents, having meetings, discussing with outside experts, convening more meetings, getting together documents to prove they are 'unteachable' and so on? If you can convince senior management that this timetabled discussion will actually save time in the future and make it easier for everyone to teach these pupils, it may eventually be possible to build it into the timetable of key staff. Schools often say 'no' to new ideas because the benefits are not made clear. You can clarify what these benefits are.

✔ Staff need to believe their feelings are listened to

When we are dealing with very troubled and vulnerable children, we need to have somewhere to offload our own feelings and fears. Schools can set this up with peer support, but it can be helpful to look for an outside facilitator as well. This could be an external consultant, someone such as an educational psychologist or psychotherapist, or by arrangement with an outside agency such as CAMHS, who might provide an experienced facilitator. Sometimes using the time of other professionals can be a more productive way forward than buying in individual sessions with children.

> *A school employed an outside consultant to have one-to-one coaching meetings with key members of staff. The results of these meetings were confidential, and the content different for different staff.*
>
> *Questions were raised about the cost of these meetings and what was going on in them, but the Head was adamant that this kind of emotional support was part of on-going professional development. It was quite separate from performance management, meeting with Local Authority advisors and line management.*
>
> *The staff involved became key members in taking the school forward, eventually joining SLT themselves. They all said it had been great to have time to think and feel listened to. Solutions to problems came from themselves, but the outside consultant enabled them to create the 'thinking space' they needed.*

✔ What the individual teacher can do

As with the example of timetabled meetings about pupils, these meetings for staff allowed thinking time which cut down on the time staff spent later on ineffective strategies and feelings of frustration. This type of group does not have to be set up by senior management. Most schools have people such as counsellors, educational psychologists and other people such as learning mentors who have some training in this type of facilitation. They may be happy to be involved in a support group or to give advice about how to do it. Be pro-active, and find out who does this in your school. Do not be afraid to ask. It will benefit you and your pupils in the long-term and is not a waste of time.

Change does not have to start at the top. It can develop from a group of individuals getting together to improve their own situations with the children and young people they are finding 'unteachable'. It can come from a department or a year group, or a group of teachers interested in a topic such as emotional literacy. In every school there will be a group, no matter how small, of people who would be prepared to start something like this if someone just suggested it, somebody who is prepared to think about the unconscious processes that might be at work.

You are not alone. Accepting or offering help should not be seen as a judgement on competence.

The manager of an LSU in a busy secondary was trying to get a coherent approach to working with certain young people. He decided to invite key staff to a lunchtime meeting and to provide the sandwiches!

This small gesture meant he could get more people together than previously. He kept the focus of each meeting on what was working, what might be driving particular behaviour, and who might be prepared to act as a mentor. He was also able to get a link person from each department to agree to liaise with him about the pupils in the unit.

✔ Team up with like-minded people

Our tendency can be to focus on what is not working, on those staff who are not interested in our ideas, who think very differently to us and seem to want to block any different ways of thinking. Focus on those who do appear to think like you, who seem prepared to think about these things. A staff group can be two people setting aside fifteen minutes to talk about a particular child and the effects on them and their teaching. Positive energy attracts others. Choose who you talk to at lunchtime. It will affect your mood for the afternoon, and possibly beyond!

✔ Take time for each other

In a busy day, how much time do we really have to ask people how they are, or to take a few moments out for a real chat? It is often clear to me on training days how useful the tea-breaks are, in that they provide time for people to catch up and exchange ideas and experiences. Staff meetings could sometimes start with a quick check-in on the state/feelings of members. Five minutes spent on this at the start can be a huge relief, and help people relax before getting onto the 'business' (incidentally, if this five minutes seems in danger of taking over, it might be an indication that your school needs to give more time to the emotional needs of the staff).

✔ Allow people to make mistakes

Develop a climate where you can be kind to yourself, where it is understood that you do not need to be perfect, where staff are not afraid to admit to mistakes or that they need help. This kind of atmosphere can be encouraged with specific use of language. For example, use phrases such as -

"OK, this has gone wrong, what can we do about it?"

"What needs to happen to make this better?"

"What can we learn from this?"

This will create a better learning climate than blame-laden language such as -

"Who did this?" "Whose fault was it?" " What's the problem?"

Learning takes place when we get things wrong. How did we learn to walk? We fell over a lot, on the way to finding out how to keep our balance. If at some time in our life someone had said, *"Don't get up until you can do it perfectly"*, we would not have learned to walk at all. Somehow in schools this idea of how learning really works disappears in the pressure for results, league tables and evaluations. A change of thinking can be started by one person challenging their own beliefs and recognising that trying to be perfect is actually stressful and counter-productive. In my experience, if one person begins to be more honest about how they feel, other people feel relieved and someone will agree!

✔ Develop the ability to give 'clean' feedback

It can be difficult to be honest with colleagues. We do not want to risk angry confrontations or hurting their feelings. However, when working with these 'difficult to teach' children and young people, it is vital to be able to give honest feedback to each other, and to them. As with our work with children, it can be useful to separate out our description of a behaviour and the interpretation we have made of it. For example, I might say:

> *"When you came in and sat down without looking at me, I interpreted that as you being annoyed at being here'"*

> This is different to -
> *"You obviously don't want to be here. Why?"*

The second version includes my own value judgements; in the first statement I have tried to separate these out. When we misunderstand each other or feel aggrieved with colleagues, it is often because of this mixing up of behaviour and interpretation.

✔ Develop a group of emotionally literate student leaders

All students need to learn how to be leaders and deal with emotions effectively. Pupils need to be allowed to aspire to something, and then have the training gap filled. If the gap is in social, emotional or behavioural skills, provide this type of training. Allow all pupils to apply for leadership positions, such as peer mentors. Show them that past misdemeanours do not count against them, and that they have a chance to learn new skills to help them be a positive member of the school.

The type of children and young people who are always in trouble are often not allowed to develop better leadership skills. They need to be given the opportunity to belong in a more positive way to the school community. They do not need to take on the more challenging leadership roles at first, but ways can be found to include them in a pro-active way. Students can, for example, become student-researchers, and look at different types of learning styles in use in different subjects. Allowing them to work collaboratively with staff is also a part of emotional literacy (*for more ideas on improving Emotional Literacy, see* Weare, 2003).

Students take the lead

A school decided to widen its body of prefects and give each group responsibility for one strand of the school development plan. The group who were looking at improving behaviour asked to take part in a staff training day on behaviour. The Headteacher agreed, as he believed it was in the spirit of collaborative working with students. However, many staff were upset, as they did not want students in their staff group.

The Headteacher had several heated meeting with these members of staff. He had to admit that he should have consulted them and explained his thinking before agreeing with the students. His comment to me was "The trouble with this Emotional Literacy thing, Marie, is that you have to listen to something you think is rubbish and then take it on board as a valid feeling from a member of staff!"

The pros and cons were discussed and a compromise was reached, where the prefects attended certain parts of the meeting which were relevant to the student body.

✔ Have open staff discussion groups which reflect on feelings

Staff need time too

A school started a leadership group for newly promoted staff. It was felt that these staff had the potential for leadership but were not moving into carrying out the roles independently. At the first meeting they carried out a SWOT analysis (Strengths, Weaknesses, Opportunities and Threats) on themselves. Out of this discussion came some very real issues about their feelings. In particular, they felt concerned about dealing with staff members who had only recently been colleagues. They felt that some staff thought they were too young and were being paid too much too soon. This was leading to feelings of guilt and extreme anxiety.

The group did not need management 'strategies' as such, they needed time to process their fears, worries and concerns on an emotional and beliefs level. They were able to share their concerns and learn from each other, as well as from more senior staff who were prepared to join the group and share their experiences.

✔ A thought for the day/week with staff as well as pupils

It may seem a bit 'Californian' to some of us, but choosing to have a motivating, inspiring, thought or learning for the day can be very positive. Staffrooms can be very cynical places, where one way of coping with the stresses is to be negative and use sarcasm. This can have a cathartic effect, but it can also be very unhelpful. Deciding for example, that the key learning for the week is to do a random act of kindness can transform even the most jaded group. In fact, use the strategies you use on demoralised pupils on yourselves. Catch yourselves being good!

✔ Be aware of unconscious defence mechanisms at work in organisations

Be on the alert for examples of splitting, omnipotence, sibling rivalry and envy in your organisation. As we have seen, schools need to be emotional and physical 'containers'. Often overwhelming feelings 'leak' out, meaning that we think we have suppressed them, but that they will come out in some way. Imagine a pressure cooker where we cannot see what is going on inside, but steam is escaping all the time! This is inevitable, but a well-timed comment or wondering aloud can work in meetings with colleagues and other adults as well as it might with children and young people. Saying something like *"It can be very difficult to think about these children"*, or *"There's a lot of anxiety around this child"* may encourage a different way of thinking in the most difficult meetings.

> *The systems in schools can sometimes sabotage our work with children. Unwittingly, we can be affected by unconscious defence mechanisms. For example, when I have worked with Learning Mentors in schools, there have sometimes been problems with rooms not being made available for individual work. The school management might have committed to the*

work on the conscious level, but at some level it is hard to give these difficult children a special time, which perhaps we would all like to have for ourselves. I have been told by Headteachers in my search for rooms that "Well, we would all like some private, individual therapy time and we don't get it!" This is an interesting example of unconscious envy and spoiling at work, developed outside conscious awareness.

✔ Bringing ideas from primary into secondary

Circle Time is a good example of something which is commonly run in primary, and not so widespread in secondary. Children do not give up the need to have a space to reflect after the age of eleven: in fact it might become more worthwhile than ever (*for good examples of how to run such groups in secondary school, see Mosley,* 1996).

I have found the following topics can be a useful focus for secondary Circle Time:

→ learning styles, and how we all learn differently
→ games which develop key learning and play skills, such as focus or concentration
→ empathy drama games, such as role-plays where students take it in turns to play different perspectives
→ drama with voice-overs, where students speculate about what a character is thinking in comparison to what they are doing
→ games such as *'Follow the Leader'* and *'Wink Murder'* which develop skills of observation, co-operation and rapport.

✓ Notice when you are doing more of what does not work

Remember that when things go wrong we tend to do more of the same. If a child is not behaving, we exclude them for ever increasing periods of time or we put them into isolation for longer periods. In fact, if something isn't working, we need to do something different - anything, but not more of the same. Bring this way of thinking into your work and your school.

In summary

Schools can be emotional and physical containers. Taking a whole-school approach to understanding behaviour and paying attention to possible unconscious processes can develop 'thinking spaces' both for teachers as well as vulnerable children and young people.

- Thinking spaces need to be created. This can be done through collaborative support groups such as those advocated by Gerda Hanko (1999), through supervision by outside consultants, or across departments, meetings around a particular child or young person. Include time to talk about the feelings of staff involved with working with these challenging pupils
- Focus on what is working rather than what is going wrong. Share the experience and do more of it

(continues ...)

- Share the emotional learning with pupils. For example, develop pupils as leaders and share the feelings about leadership with them, as well as the more obvious behavioural strategies

- Develop a leadership process where senior staff are encouraged to discuss their own feelings, for example on issues of moving into leadership

- Suggest whole-school ideas for staff to use in developing the Emotional Literacy of students. For example, if you have a weekly staff bulletin or noticeboard, have a thought for the week for everyone to focus on with their pupils, for example, "*Show empathy with others*" "*Be kind to others*" "*Use good listening skills*". All staff should then take every opportunity to 'catch students being good' and doing this

- Be prepared to admit to your failures as well as your successes. See these failures as opportunities for learning. Show that everyone is human

- Use the start of meetings to focus on any unconscious anxieties. Even five minutes discussing what is uppermost in your mind can help relieve some anxieties and bring the focus back to the task

- Be aware of unconscious defence mechanisms such as envy and spoiling which might begin to operate in moments of stress around teaching certain pupils

- Build in planned, time-tabled meetings for key staff to discuss the needs of the most challenging children and young people. It will save time in the long-run

- Practise assertive communication, not aggressive or passive. Develop the art of 'clean feedback', in which you separate out a description of a behaviour and what you infer from it

- Use Circle Time techniques in secondary as well as primary school

- Develop a common vocabulary which re-frames behaviour in an attempt to understand what might be driving or what it might be showing us. Ask, for example, *"What is the child's need?"* *"What do we want?"*
"What might be going on here underneath the surface?"
"How does this make you feel?"

Chapter 12

And finally...

PUTTING IT ALL TOGETHER

So, coming back to the questions posed at the beginning of the book, how can we make best use of understanding and insights from the world of therapy, to inform our teaching and help some of these very hard-to-reach young people? I hope the preceding chapters have provided you with some fresh ideas. There is no magic formula for succeeding with these pupils in the classroom, and there will be times when we will feel overwhelmed by the task and want to give up. However, if we can incorporate therapeutic thinking into our everyday teaching and learning, I believe we can still make a difference to these 'unteachables'. Sometimes the difference will not be immediate. We might never see progress ourselves, but in my experience, there is a great value for these children and young people in being surrounded by adults who take time to try to think about them and hold them in mind.

Recently, I met a boy I had struggled to teach for three years in secondary. Eventually he had been given an alternative timetable. He insisted on coming over to me, when I was doing my shopping, and said:

> *"Hello, Miss. Guess what, I'm working doing painting and decorating now and living with my girlfriend. Don't know why you ever bothered with me at school, but thanks for not giving up ... didn't believe it at the time, but I did need help!"*

This is an example of a boy who will not have appeared in any of the school's academic results, but he was very keen to assure me that we had made a difference to his life. That is what teachers can do, and it's important we remember that.

In summary

You might have noticed that this book is not really about adding to a long list of teaching strategies. My aim has been to show that we can add to our repertoire simply by taking on some extra knowledge, from a different viewpoint.

I strongly believe that the key to working with these 'unteachable' children is to shift our ways of thinking and to remember the huge importance teachers can play in children's lives. Curiosity is a key state for learning. You do not need to have all the answers and solutions to problems. But if you are prepared to get curious and explore with the young person, to 'get alongside them' and into their map of the world, you will be allowing a space for thinking that is not often available in a packed curriculum. Our schools today need to show young people how to develop, nurture and repair relationships, and to recognise that this is the key not only to good learning environments, but also to managing successfully in their wider lives and in society.

I am not saying it is easy. I have had my own fair share of disasters. I have, for example, tried my best with kids who, minutes after leaving my room, have gone back to class and done something inexcusable. I have been called names, I have had parents refuse to work with me, I have upset staff, I have indeed at times upset myself - all in my search to work with these supposedly 'unteachable' children.

I do not have all the answers, but I do have a belief that schools and staff in school are the best chance these children have to experience thinking and being thought about. None of us can wave a magic wand, and make life better for these children and the adults who deal with them, on our own. That is why teachers and therapists need to work together, think together and learn from each other. You are part of your students' best chance. We need to strive to create these thinking spaces. We need to maintain our capacity to think around these pupils, so that they have the chance to learn relationship skills which they may have missed out on in their earlier, often chaotic, life experiences.

I would like to end with a quotation from Virginia Satir, a renowned family therapist, who talks about working towards a system where the Five Freedoms are respected. If we can be part of learning environments which allow all of us - staff, colleagues from other agencies, parents and children, to have these freedoms, we will create situations where we can really work with 'unteachable' children and young people, and support each other in doing so.

The Five Freedoms

The freedom to see and hear what is here instead of what should be, was, or will be
The freedom to say what one feels and thinks, instead of what one should
The freedom to feel what one feels, instead of what one ought
The freedom to ask for what one wants, instead of always waiting for permission
The freedom to take risks on one's own behalf, instead of
choosing to be only 'secure' and not rock the boat (Satir, 1976)

References

Barrett, M. & Trevitt, J. (1991) *Attachment Behaviour and the Schoolchild* London: Routledge

Bion, W. R. (1962) A theory of thinking International Journal of Psycho-Analysis, Vol.43: Reprinted in Second Thoughts: *Selected Papers on Psychoanalysis* (Maresfield Library)(1984) London: Karnac Books

Bomber, L.M. (2007) *Inside I'm Hurting: Practical strategies for supporting children with attachment difficulties in schools* London: Worth Publishing

Bowlby, J. (1988) *A Secure Base: Clinical Applications of Attachment Theory* London: Routledge

Edgcumbe, R. (2000) *Anna Freud: A View of Development, Disturbance and Therapeutic Techniques* London: Routledge

Freud, A. (1973) *Normality and Pathology in Childhood* London: Hogarth and Penguin

Geddes, H. (2006) *Attachment in the Classroom: The links between children's early experience, emotional well-being and performance in school* London: Worth Publishing

Gerhardt, S. (2004) *Why Love Matters: How Affection Shapes a Baby's Brain* Sussex: Brunner-Routledge

Gray, P. & Panter, S. (2000) Exclusion or inclusion: Perspectives on policy in England for pupils with emotional and behavioural difficulties *Support for Learning* Vol. 15 (1), 4-7

Hadfield, J. (1992) *Classroom Dynamics: A Resource book for teachers* Oxford: Oxford University Press

Hanko, G. (1999) *Increasing Competence Through Collaborative Problem Solving* London: David Fulton

McDermott, I. & O'Connor, J. (2001) *Thorson's Way of NLP* London: Thorsons

Mosley, J. (1996) *Quality Circle Time in the Secondary School* London: David Fulton

Prochaska, J., Norcross, J. & DiClemente, C. (1994) *Changing for Good: The revolutionary program that explains the six stages of change and teaches you how to free yourself from bad habits* New York: W. Morrow

Revell, J., Norman, S. & Peet, M. (1997) *In Your Hands: NLP in ELT* London: Saffire Press

Rinvolucri, M. & Davis, P. (1995) *More Grammar Games: Cognitive, affective and movement activities for EFL students* Cambridge: Cambridge University Press

Rinvolucri, M. & Davis, P. (1990) *The Confidence Book* (Pilgrims Longman Resource Books) London: Longman

Rogers, B. (2006) *Cracking the Hard Class: Strategies for Managing the Harder than Average Class*, 2nd Edn. London: Paul Chapman Publishing

Satir, V. (1976) *Making Contact* Celestial Arts: Millbrae, CA

Schore, A.N. (2001) The effects of a secure attachment relationship on right brain development, affect regulation and infant mental health *Infant Mental Health Journal*, 22, pp. 7-66

Sunderland, M. (1999) *A Pea Called Mildred: A story to help children pursue their hopes and dreams* Milton Keynes: Speechmark Publishing

Sunderland, M. (2001) *Willy and the Wobbly House: A story for children who are anxious or obsessional* Milton Keynes: Speechmark Publishing

Visser, J. & Rayner, S. (Eds.) (1999) Emotional and Behavioural Difficulties: A reader Lichfield: QED

Ward, I. (Ed.) (1995) *The Psychology of Nursery Education* London: Karnac Books

Winnicott, D.W. (1971) *Playing and Reality* London: Routledge